The Tertiary Sector

Education 16 – 19 in Schools and Colleges

Maurice Holt

with contributions by
Richard Pring and Richard Whitfield

HODDER AND STOUGHTON
LONDON SYDNEY AUCKLAND TORONTO

British Library Cataloguing In Publication Data
Holt, Maurice
   The tertiary sector
   1. Education, Secondary—England
   2. Vocational education—England
   I. Title.   II. Pring, Richard
   III. Whitfield, Richard Charles
   373.2'38'0942   LA635

ISBN 0 340 25515 3 Boards   NIS
ISBN 0 340 25516 1 Unibook

Printed in Great Britain for Hodder and Stoughton Educational,
a division of Hodder and Stoughton Ltd,
Mill Road, Dunton Green, Sevenoaks, Kent,
by Biddles Ltd, Guildford, Surrey

Contents

Preface

This book has its origins in the concern of sixth-form staff to keep track of changes in 16–19 education: of the courses and examinations that are available, the different kinds of institution that exist and the new curriculum strategies that are evolving.

The concern took shape at the Cambridge Institute of Education in 1977, and led to my directing later that year, on behalf of the Institute, a residential course on the subject of the sixth form: problems and perspectives, ideals and expediencies. The conference was repeated in 1978. One result was some useful data on the arrangements in the sixth forms of the participating schools, and on the views of sixth-form staff. I refer to these in the text from time to time.

Another result was a strong feeling that information about developments in 16–19 education was scattered among a variety of sources, and that it would be helpful to bring it together and put sixth-form education in a wider perspective. This book is an attempt to do this.

Professor Richard Whitfield gave the opening address to the first conference, and Professor Richard Pring to the second. It is therefore appropriate that their respective contributions on those occasions should be reflected in Chapters 4 and 2 of this book.

Public and professional interest in 16–19 education has grown since 1977. The Schools Council's N and F proposals have been aired again, leading to much discussion and argument, and have been finally abandoned. Government initiatives to ease youth unemployment have made for greater anomalies between education and training, and calls for a national inquiry and a better coordinated system of tertiary education have come from many directions. The prospect of falling rolls in the early 1980s brings with it the risk that educational considerations may take second place to economic necessities unless proper preparations are begun soon.

This book, therefore, is a contribution to a debate which has been with us since the early sixties but which is still unresolved. I hope that, in attempting to take a wider view and examine underlying curriculum questions, it will help to indicate the lines along which a unified tertiary sector might develop.

A word is perhaps necessary about this book's structure. The initial chapter has outlined the general background, looked at historical influences, briefly noted some approaches in other countries, and stressed the importance of the 11–16 sector on tertiary education. It has pointed to some unifying issues, and these will be a recurrent theme in later chapters.

In the next chapter, Richard Pring discusses, from the point of view of a philosopher of education, some of the concepts like breadth and relevance which are central to the 16–19 curriculum. He looks in particular at the idea of curriculum balance in the context of tertiary education. Chapter 3 examines the link between the traditional sixth-form curriculum and its system of examinations, and the various attempts that have been made to reform this system in the interests of curriculum breadth. Provision for one-year sixth formers is also discussed.

In Chapter 4, Richard Whitfield argues the case for a broad 11–16 curriculum as the essential preliminary to greater tertiary breadth, and sets out the essentials of such a scheme based on a concept of balance which differs from that advanced by Pring. But in suggesting a differential approach to balance in the tertiary sector, Whitfield and Pring end up at a roughly similar position, with Pring suggesting more strongly the importance of method rather than content. Whitfield goes on to discuss the usefulness of the International Baccalaureate as a scheme which offers both breadth and depth, and looks in particular at sixth-form general studies schemes and the place of the Theory of Knowledge paper in the International Baccalaureate course.

Chapter 5 looks at the distinctive elements which make up the traditional sixth-form curriculum, and the ways in which schools are adapting to current problems of courses and resources. Provision for general studies courses is discussed, and schemes for linking sixth-forms with each other or with other tertiary institutions are examined. In Chapter 6 the development of sixth-form and tertiary colleges is traced, and their distinctive curricular approaches are discussed.

Chapter 7 looks in some detail at the scope of modular courses, and the extent to which devices of this kind might be applicable to tertiary education. It concludes with a review of the problems facing schools and colleges in the future and suggests some short-term expedients, and some longer-term strategies.

Devon, 1979   M.H.

Contributors

Mr Maurice Holt was formerly the first Headmaster of Sheredes School, Hertfordshire, and is now an Education and Curriculum Consultant.

Professor Richard Pring is a Professor of Education at the University of Exeter.

Professor Richard Whitfield is Head of the Department of Educational Enquiry at the University of Aston in Birmingham.

Acknowledgments

My thanks must go first to the Cambridge Institute of Education, and in particular to its director, Joyce Skinner, its secretary, John Child, and its assistant secretary for courses and conferences, Sue Anderson. Without their initiative and support neither this book, nor the conferences from which it grew, would have come about. Their encouragement, indeed, extends beyond the confines of 16–19 education and I am delighted to be able to acknowledge it here.

I owe a further debt to other participants in the original conferences: to their members and staff, and to those who made salient contributions. I must thank Peter Bryan, secretary of the Cambridge Collegiate Board, for his outline of the Board's functions in Appendix A, and Philip Merfield, principal of Exeter College, for his summary of the college's provision in Appendix B. Brian Holley made valuable contributions to both conferences, and I am grateful to him for some useful suggestions regarding the scope of modular courses. My discussions with Patrick Nobes have been stimulating and fruitful.

It has been a pleasure to work with my collaborators, Professor Richard Pring and Professor Richard Whitfield. I alone, however, bear responsibility for any inadequacies in the rest of the book. I am grateful to Stanley Foster, of Hodder and Stoughton, for his help in seeing this book through to completion, and to Professor Denis Lawton, Deputy Director of the University of London Institute of Education, for his valuable comments on the manuscript.

The heads of several schools, and the principals of a number of sixth-form and tertiary colleges, were good enough to allow me to visit their establishments and talk to staff and students. My thanks go to all of them, and particularly to John Miles, principal of Bridgwater College, who not only contributed to the 1978 conference, but also kindly read the manuscript and made a number of useful suggestions.

1
Unifying Issues in 16–19 Education

As soon as we start to think about 16–19 education as a separate and distinct stage in the educational sequence, we notice how difficult it is to give it a distinctive character. It lacks the prescriptive associations of the secondary school, as much as the liberated culture of university or polytechnic. We are tempted to define it not as an entity in its own right, but as whatever fills the educational space between the end of compulsory education and the start of adult options. It has the same inchoate, shadowy formlessness as the middle school—a grey area sandwiched between established landmarks. Even the 16–19 age-range term used to describe this sector of education has its revisionists. The 1979 White Paper produced in the last months of the Callaghan government is called *Education and Training for 16–18 Year Olds*, and offers statistics on this basis; but the *General Household Survey*, published by the Central Statistical Office a little later the same year, sticks to the 16–19 bracket.

Although the 16–19 sector might appear indeterminate to the administrators, it has a definite reality for its student clients. It is a time when critical choices are made: choices between courses and qualifications, and between different institutional providers. The 16–19 stage may lead to a job, or to more education; it may be full or part-time; and it has its own paradoxes to offer. Thus a vocational-sounding course at a further education college might cover a wider area of study than a more academic one, such as three science A-levels, in a school. Some courses may last for two or more years, and others for only a few weeks or months. Some require fees, while others pay students to take them. On the face of it, 16–19 education is a stage upon which generalisations fit rather uncomfortably.

For many school leavers 16–19 education or training has no appeal at all. This may be due to lack of ambition, or of suitable courses, or to an unfortunate experience of compulsory schooling. For any 16–19 student, these will be the three factors: his own personal background and interests, the nature of the course and its terminal value to him, and his educational state at the start. Whatever his decision, career options are involved. A fifth-former with a few O-levels might opt for employment and an apprenticeship rather than two years on an Ordinary National Diploma

(OND) or Technician Education Council (TEC) national diploma course at a further education college. Choices of this kind can be crucial if the student is to lead a fulfilled life, and if our society is to develop in the directions we assign to it. There is an uncertainty here, though: how far does 16–19 education belong to the more general aims of secondary school, and how far to the personal and economic aims of adult life?

The uncertainty is reflected in the other terms used to describe 16–19 education. Upper secondary education, or second-cycle secondary education, are terms which stress the secondary link and the context of the 11–18 school and its sixth form. But in 1977–8, according to the 1979 White Paper, only 14 per cent of 16–18 year olds in England and Wales were taking courses in schools leading to GCE A-level. And most schools take pains to provide separate units for their sixth formers, so as to acknowledge the more expansive culture of the young adult. Given the variety of 16–19 educational provision, there seems little point in associating it with the ambience of compulsory schooling.

Others, with equal perversity, sometimes describe higher education so as to include at least some types of 16–19 education. It is true that the concept of higher education has become more blurred, with the emergence of colleges of higher education and a rash of new courses, many of sub-degree standard. Yet we can draw a clear line between educational programmes defined, at their upper limit, by the standard of A-level or its equivalent, and those which go on from there. And again, there is a social and cultural discontinuity; the university, polytechnic or college of higher education student has reached his majority, and his life-style is free from the constraints of bodies which, in some way or other, are *in loco parentis.* Furthermore, to see 16–19 education as an aspect of higher education makes it that much harder to view it as a whole and pick out—as I hope to do in this chapter—any unifying ideas which might help us give some shape to its diversity.

Some currency has been given to the term *post-compulsory education* to describe 16–19 provision. But it can describe so much more than this, and ought to, if it is to be worth having: it covers adult education, training courses for union officials, vocational re-training, all the way to higher education. It is a convenient way of describing all those educational options, beyond the statutory school-leaving age, which an advanced society might set before its citizens. For some, they will be full-time post-16 courses for five years or more; for others, nothing more than an evening class in yoga when the children reach school age. As a description of 16–19 education, it is free from the exclusive associations of 'upper-secondary' or 'higher'; the trouble is that it is not exclusive enough.

There is much to be said for appropriating the term *tertiary education* as a description of that sector which deals chiefly with 16–19 year olds, which carries on from where compulsory schooling leaves off but which stops at the point where post-18 higher education, or what the Department of Education and Science (DES) calls 'advanced further education', begins. 'Tertiary education' has a positive ring which 'non-advanced further education' lacks, and it completes the logic of the primary, secondary and tertiary stages. It means that we can look at a group of students of similar age and sharing the same cultural territory, albeit with many different interests and aspirations, while recognising that some of their courses will attract adult students. Then tertiary education will go on in schools alongside secondary education, and in FE and tertiary colleges alongside other adult education. But it will be the sole concern of sixth-form colleges.

A historical perspective

Now that we have dealt with the nomenclature, let us take a closer look at the tertiary sector to see what patterns emerge. At first sight, the prospect is daunting:

> Beyond sixteen the picture . . . is one of great confusion—a veritable jungle of institutions which differ widely in status, in resources, and in the opportunities . . . which they can offer to their students (Pedley 1977).

In plainer terms, *The Times Educational Supplement*—which has done much to draw attention to the shortcomings of 16–19 provision—sees 'a sort of cluttered supermarket where excellent bargains jostle for space with dubious buys but where nothing is clearly labelled' (18.11.77). Our first task must be to consider how this state of affairs has come about.

As with most aspects of English education, we find ourselves in the shadow of the nineteenth century and, in particular, of a divided structure. Just as a clear line runs from the Victorian public schools to the maintained grammar schools of the post-war years, and from the elementary schools to the secondary moderns, so the distinction in the tertiary sector between academic education in schools and vocational education in further education (FE) colleges is part of the same pattern. And as a rule, government interest in scientific and technical education is aroused only by fears of foreign competition and economic weakness. While academic education is seen as self-justifying, technical education is an instrumental activity, linked essentially with vocation and trade.

The key point here is that when the provisions of the 1902 Balfour Act for maintained grammar schools were implemented, the Permanent Secretary to the Board of Education, Sir Robert Morant, took pains to ensure that they followed a curriculum pattern already established in the public schools. As a result, not only did school sixth forms reinforce the tradition of specialisation prior to university entry; the insecure foothold secured by science and the performance subjects in the main-school curriculum remained tenuous. This was a narrow interpretation of a liberal education, and stemmed largely from the dominance of the classics. Although science found its way on to the public school curriculum as the nineteenth century wore on, it was as a 'science side'. The 'classical side' remained separate and tended to attract the ablest scholars. In due course, modern languages and history made up a 'modern side', and so the influence of these new subjects was not so much to extend the basic curriculum, as to partition it.

The effect of this on the sixth form curriculum—traditionally, the academic part of the tertiary sector—will be traced in more detail in Chapter 3. We need only note that the pattern of pre-university specialisation has proved astonishingly durable, and has so far defied all efforts to change it. Between the wars, the Higher Schools Certificate expressly forbade, for many years, a choice of subjects that bridged the arts-science divide; the advent of GCE A-level in 1950 gave scope for a wider mix, but the notion of 'study in depth' was well entrenched, and sanctified by the Crowther Report of 1959. The Schools Council has been committed, since its foundation in 1964, to broadening the sixth-form curriculum. But after thirteen years of non-stop committee work, its N and F-level proposals were given a lukewarm reception and eventually rejected, to no one's surprise, by the new 1979 Conservative administration.

To follow the growth of technical education—traditionally, the vocational part of the tertiary sector—we must first give credit to the 1875 Report of the Devonshire Commission on Scientific Instruction and the Advancement of Science, which declared (Maclure 1965):

> . . . the present state of Scientific Instruction in our Schools is extremely unsatisfactory. The omission from a Liberal Education of a great branch of Intellectual Culture is of itself a matter for serious regret; and considering the increasing importance of Science to the Material Interests of the Country, we cannot but regard its almost total exclusion from the training of the upper and middle classes as little less than a national misfortune.

There is much to support the view that our economic decline stems in large part from a neglect of the practical arts, and that it has been going on for over a century. For the Devonshire Report's advice went unheeded, and the Samuelson Report of 1884 on Technical Instruction focused specifically on 'the industrial classes' at home and abroad, as a result of increasing foreign competition. By this time the Mechanics' Institutes founded earlier in the century had been joined by a variety of trade schools, and the City of London livery companies had founded the City and Guilds of London Institute (CGLI): indeed, the country's first technical college had opened at

Finsbury Park in 1883. The Samuelson Commission had little alternative but to recommend 'the establishment and maintenance of secondary and technical schools and colleges' by local authorities, and of schools 'in which the study of natural science, drawing, mathematics and modern languages shall take the place of Latin and Greek'.

Up to this critical point, the option was still open to make science and the applied arts equal elements of a broad curriculum. After it, vested interests would ensure that one road led to the universities via an 'academic' curriculum, and the other to a variety of technical institutions by a great variety of routes. And within technical institutions, as Gordon and Lawton (1978) remark, the chance was lost to link science education with technical education: 'as time went on technical education became associated with vocational training of a limited kind and secondary schools concentrated on "pure" science, mainly chemistry and physics'. This divided view is reflected today in the existence of two quite separate sets of regulations for students of the same age who might be taking the same A-level subjects: school regulations if they are in sixth forms or sixth-form colleges, and further education regulations if they are in an FE or tertiary college.

By 1901, advanced scientific and other teaching had developed in the upper forms of some urban elementary schools. It was declared illegal by the Cockerton Judgment of that year, which ruled that such extensions of elementary education were a misappropriation of public funds. The effect of establishing the Balfour/Morant grammar schools under the 1902 Act as the official form of secondary education was to squeeze out this development of a broader curriculum, and reinforce the separation between the grammar and elementary school traditions. The county and county borough councils replaced the school boards as the local authorities, and extended the technical college provision as funds permitted. The economic climate of the twenties and thirties was a considerable constraint, and the Hadow/Spens doctrine emerged, in the reports of 1926 and 1938, as a further refinement of the divided system. Alongside the traditional grammar schools, 'modern' schools were proposed with less formal teaching methods; and 'a new type of higher school of technical character' was to be established, with parity of esteem between all three forms of secondary education.

The technical high school never really caught on, despite its endorsement by the Norwood Committee in 1943 and the post-war attempts to establish a tripartite structure. It was killed partly by the suspicions of parents, who saw both it and the modern school as a second and third best to the grammar school; partly by the extra expense involved, which confined it, in the main, to the more committed urban areas; and partly, too, by the hostility of the grammar schools, who saw it as a threat to their supply of able pupils, and one with perhaps an increasing appeal at a time when the successes of wartime technology were very evident. So the bipartite system continued until comprehensive schools began to prevail in the sixties, and the needs of technical education were met by the post-war growth of the FE colleges.

The 1944 Education Act expressly charged local authorities with 'the provision for their area of adequate facilities for further education', and they were required to prepare appropriate schemes to offer not only full and part-time post-school education, but also 'leisure-time occupation'. The long-term intention was to offer tertiary education for all to the age of 18, ultimately on a day-release or block-release basis at 'county colleges'; attendance would be compulsory for those who had left school and were not attending other further education classes.

The total attendance time for this compulsory part-time tertiary education was to be 330 hours per year—just ten hours more than had been specified in the similar provisions of the 1918 Education Act, which followed German practice and proposed 'part-time day continuation schools'. The slump after the First World War put paid to these good intentions, and although the 1959 Crowther Report attempted to breathe new life into the county college provision of the 1944 Act, economic difficulties after the Second World War pushed it further down the list of priorities. Instead, full-time technical education expanded dramatically, and some part-time growth followed. Between 1951 and 1965, the number of full-time FE students grew from 55 to 202 thousand; the corresponding part-time increase was only from 1900 to 2800 thousand. The 1956 White Paper on Technical Education opens with a quotation from the Prime Minister, Sir Anthony Eden, which reflects the mood of the times: 'Those (countries) with the best systems of education will win . . . We shall need many more scientists, engineers and technicians.' The White Paper recognised the haphazard way in which technical provision had grown to meet local conditions, and attempted to rationalise things to some extent. Levels of technical education were defined, sandwich courses came about, the number of day-release students almost doubled between 1954 and 1964, and specialist facilities were provided, including more technical teacher-training colleges.

All this energetic, demand-based development received a further boost in the 1961 White Paper, which re-defined the scope of courses at the lower level, and promoted closer consultation between examining bodies, colleges and industry. Craft courses were broadened to prevent premature specialisation, and closer links grew up between schools and technical colleges. Increasing national affluence fuelled the demand for skills and qualifications, and between 1963 and 1970, for example, the number of full-time teachers in further education increased by 75 per cent. The sheer variety of FE courses increased, too, despite the rationalisations of the two

White Papers, the efforts of Regional Advisory Councils and attempts by local authorities to get closer inter-college cooperation. By 1972, Cantor and Roberts could look at the colleges, and remark:

> Even more complex is the variety of courses they offer. These may consist of different subjects at varying levels of ability, leading to different qualifications for a wide range of jobs . . . While such variety provides greater educational opportunities than ever before for the student, it will almost certainly baffle him by its complexity.

The Haslegrave Report of 1969 was a further attempt to tidy up the examination system, for the 1961 White Paper had led to a luxuriant growth in National Certificate and City and Guilds courses. Its recommendations have been implemented by the establishment of the TEC in 1973, and of the Business Education Council (BEC) in the following year. These bodies are developing new courses and examinations at various levels, so that, although the differing structure of the TEC Diploma prevents a direct comparison with the old OND, it will have 'the same currency for the purpose of qualifying the student to proceed to degree and comparable courses of higher education' (TEC policy statement, 1974).

The two systems

It is worth noting, at this point, that an OND course is a full-time programme for two years, demanding roughly the same entry qualifications of four O-levels as a school would generally expect of an entrant to a three A-level course lasting the same time. And OND, like three satisfactory A-levels, is an acceptable entry qualification to a degree course in higher education. But there is an important difference. The school student is concerned with a *subject-based* programme; he concentrates on three, possibly four, A-level subjects, and alongside them will be offered recreational facilities and a course—which may, or may not, be examined—in general studies. The OND student takes, in contrast, a *course-based* programme; an OND course in Building includes a range of subjects, brought together by the theme of the course. As well as building technology, science, mathematics, surveying and so on, there will be a substantial general-studies element. The new TEC national diploma courses work on the same principle. This difference in the character of student programmes is a significant measure of the divergence between the two systems. Tertiary provision in schools has retained the subject basis of the 11–16 curriculum: it is, after all, even closer to the polarizing influence of university honours courses. But in further education, the key influence has been the use to which acquired knowledge is to be put. In schools, the organising device is the conceptual structure of each separate subject; in further education, the contributory subjects are subordinate to a unifying purpose or theme. This is equally true at lower levels of study. Just as less academic sixth-formers may take a group of O-Level, Certificate of Secondary Education (CSE), or Certificate of Extended Education (CEE) courses in the lower sixth, so their opposite numbers in an FE or tertiary college would tend to take BEC, TEC or City and Guilds courses in business studies, home management, hairdressing and similar courses with a vocational character.

It is, though, a sign of the times that there are two areas of overlap between these two vertical systems. One is the number of students taking A-levels at FE colleges, which increased markedly in the sixties and continues its upward trend. In 1976-7, for instance, just over 10 per cent of full-time 16-18 year old students taking A-levels were doing so in FE or tertiary colleges. In the three years from 1968 to 1971, the number of full-time A-level students in FE colleges in England and Wales rose by 40 per cent, yet in the six years from 1964 to 1970, the corresponding increase for school A-level students was only 24 per cent. DES statistics for 16 and 17 year olds, 1975-6, show that 23 per cent were receiving full-time education in schools, 10 per cent full-time education in FE colleges, and a further 27 per cent part-time education in FE colleges. The FE sector has therefore become the major provider of tertiary education. This gives a total of 60 per cent still in education, and leaves 40 per cent receiving no post-school education at all. If one takes the whole 16-19 group as the basis, the figures look even gloomier. In 1977, 29 per cent were in full-time education, 20 per cent in part-time, and 51 per cent received none at all (*General Household Survey 1977*, HMSO).

The other overlap is much more recent, and dates from the introduction of CGLI Foundation Courses in 1976. A small but growing number of schools are entering candidates for these courses, particularly as one-year courses for lower-sixth students. Each course has a vocational theme, like engineering or commercial studies, and the structure is therefore course-based and not subject based. In some cases, schools make use of nearby FE facilities for part of the programme. The important point is that the school staff involved are having to regard their subject specialisms in a new light: as means to an end, rather than an end in themselves. These matters will be examined further in later chapters.

In other European countries the post-war growth of tertiary education has been equally vigorous, and has shown the same tendency to branch off into a variety of institutions which may be competing rather than complementary. But a number of factors are peculiar to the English scene. There is, first, the reluctance of our industries to provide post-school education for their young employees. The Germans have for more than fifty years compelled all their school leavers to attend at least part-time vocational training establishments. It is difficult not to associate this parsimony with our poorer economic performance. The final attempt of the Callaghan administration to improve matters was the proposal of the consultative paper *A Better Start in Working Life* (April 1979) to offer 'traineeships', lasting several months, to one-third of the young workers who enter jobs below craft level. Initially, employers would qualify for grants to set up the programme. While the TUC has described this scheme as 'too modest', the chief training adviser for the Rubber and Plastics Processing Industry Training Board has been reported (*Education*, 27.4.79) as saying that he 'did not agree with the discussion paper's assumption that employers could be reasonably asked to foot the whole bill for the education and training of their young employees'. The proposal is, of course, now in limbo following the change of Government.

A second factor which makes us a European odd-man-out is our attachment to the idea of public examinations at 16-plus. To some extent, this can be seen as a counterbalance to our lack of central control, and the introduction of national performance testing since 1978, by means of the DES Assessment of Performance Unit (APU), suggests a desire to control schools even further. All testing has a backwash effect on the curriculum, and renders it more resistant to change. The effect of GCE and CSE has been to confine curriculum development largely to the earlier years of secondary schooling, and also to make for a sharper dividing line between the secondary and tertiary sectors. The switch from O-level spoon-feeding to A-level private study is difficult for many nascent sixth formers. By the same token, it makes it easier to establish separate tertiary institutions, and the growth of sixth-form and tertiary colleges has been striking.

A third factor is the commitment of our universities, in the main, to the three-year, single-subject honours degree course. This exerts a downward pressure on the school curriculum: it forced the grammar school into a subject-based curriculum followed by the most specialised sixth-form course in the world, and the comprehensive school has had no incentive to adopt a different approach.

All these factors have affected the rate of tertiary growth, the structure of tertiary courses, and their distribution between schools and colleges. But an overriding factor arises from the combination of a decentralised system with our reluctance (or inability) to formulate curriculum policies in education. It seems to take a war to do it: the last major reforms of 18-plus examinations took place in 1917 and 1951, and in each case they reflected post-war idealism. The central decision-making machinery in other European countries is not without its disadvantages, but it can at least help fresh thinking from first principles. Until 1977, the DES and Her Majesty's Inspectorate opted for a passive post-war role, and declined to stand up and be counted on any issue of real importance. Even when politicians have sensed the need for a new initiative (for instance, David Eccles's 1961 notion of a Curriculum Study Group), the chance has usually been fumbled. Local education authorities have concerned themselves with the minutiae of comprehensive reorganisation, and let the key curriculum questions go unasked. The domination of the Schools Council by teachers' organisations has led it to devote its energies to the launching of subject-based projects, offered to schools on a cafeteria basis: its curriculum policy is, quite explicitly, that it has no policy.

In the tertiary sector, in particular, the pattern of growth has been one of *ad hoc* solutions, followed by attempts to clear a way through the undergrowth every now and again. The method has failed dismally for schools, which still struggle to bring coherence to sixth form general studies, courses for one-year sixth formers, and A-level programmes. But it has worked rather better in further education, free from emotional interpretations of 'study in depth'. For example, the Certificate of Office Studies (COS) was first offered in 1963-4 'to meet the need for a practical and balanced programme of study for the young office worker' (Cantor and Roberts, 1972). It replaced more than 50 examinations offered by different bodies, and by 1971 over ten thousand students were taking it. Now the COS, in its turn, has given way to the BEC General Diploma. This offers a number of option modules in business education, and so takes the process of rationalisation a stage further.

Piecemeal change of this kind can re-shuffle the pieces at the operational level, but it is no substitute for the kind of higher-level planning which is necessary for the effective coordination of aims, courses and resources. The difficulty is that this involves upsetting the interests already established on the field of play. It is always easier to add something new rather than think afresh about what is already there. Thus we have school sixth forms, sixth-form centres, colleges of further education, and plain technical colleges; since 1966 we have had sixth-form colleges, and since 1970 tertiary colleges. And alongside this haphazard structure, the Manpower Services Commission (MSC) has now erected a kind of lean-to. Its Youth Opportunities Programme combines paid work experience with forms of further education, and 'is bound to provide a means for education and training to come together and provide learning which is work rather than institution based' (Holland, 1978). This initiative is a response to the growing numbers of young unemployed, and in many ways it is an imaginative programme. But it is essentially a political expedient. It raises fundamental questions about the relation between education and training, but it offers no reasoned answer to them. It had a handsome budget of £160m for the year 1978-9, and its programme of courses, project-based work experience, training workshops and community service will do something to help. In 1979 the

Manpower Services Commission is spending at an annual rate of about £600m, but it is a sad irony that attempts to do something about the 40-odd per cent of 16 year olds who leave education behind when they leave school should be made not during the years of prosperity, but as a result of an economic crisis. It is an improvisation born of bleak necessity rather than any educational ideal.

Unifying pressures

One significant result, however, of the public interest in secondary education during the seventies has been an attempt by the DES to determine such an ideal for the 11–16 curriculum. The 1977 Green Paper shows a shift of emphasis away from the consumer-choice basis of curriculum design in the fourth and fifth years of the comprehensive school, towards one which seeks to identify a common framework for all pupils: 'It is clear that the time has come to try to establish generally accepted principles for the composition of the secondary curriculum for all pupils.' The 1977 DES/HMI discussion document, *Curriculum 11–16*, calls for a common core for two-thirds of the curriculum for all children up to school-leaving age:

> In too many cases, curriculum planning has been piecemeal—a matter of trying to cope with particular situations and problems as they arise rather than of developing a coherent programme based on a carefully thought out set of objectives.

This is an important development, for it amounts to nothing less than an attempt to give an educational purpose to the comprehensive school. Although multiple-option schemes in the fourth and fifth years are ostensibly an aid to pupil motivation through choice, it is a choice which may be educationally harmful:

> The freedom to stop studying history, or art, or music, or biology at 14 means that pupils are not being given the introduction to their own cultural inheritance to which we believe they have a right.

The case for curriculum breadth has, of course, been argued for some time by educationists. Hirst (1965) took the concept of a liberal education as its basis, and White (1973) proposed a similar scheme as the basis of a compulsory curriculum. Lawton (1973) advanced further the idea of a curriculum based on a 'selection from the culture', first mooted by Raymond Williams (1961), and in 1971 a curriculum based on a concept of disciplines was described by Whitfield. A few comprehensive schools have developed forms of a common curriculum.

The Inspectorate's advocacy of a common 11–16 curriculum based on cultural experience reveals altogether broader support for change, and it is reasonable to suppose that the 1980s will see the secondary curriculum moving steadily in this direction. This has implications for the tertiary sector in two respects. First, the expectation that all 16 year olds will have completed a broad course of studies would offer tertiary institutions a common input for course planning. This is not to suppose a nationally-imposed common curriculum; indeed, I have argued elsewhere (Holt 1979) that school-based curriculum planning offers the only realistic way forward. There would also be very great variations in the degree and extent of pupils' understanding. All the same, the knowledge that all pupils had been given experience of key concepts in aesthetic, social, scientific and other cultural forms would be a distinct advance on the present state of things. These points are discussed further by Richard Whitfield in Chapter 4.

Second, it is likely that the tendency to see the 11–16 curriculum as one aiming at broad experience will have a 'knock-on' effect in the tertiary sector. Increasing attention will be given to the case for maintaining breadth in the 16–19 curriculum: possibly to a search for the Green Paper's 'generally accepted principles' for such a curriculum, or at any rate to attempts to bring a more coherent shape to 16–19 education. There have already been some signs of this. In 1976, for example, the June issue of the DES house journal *Trends in Education* called for 'a unified approach to educational preparation' in the 16–19 sector:

> There is a growing recognition that training for jobs at all levels needs to be supplemented by a wider education, albeit with a practical flavour, to provide the groundwork for life-long learning.

And the Organisation for Economic Cooperation and Development (OECD) study *Beyond Compulsory Schooling* (1976) notes a widespread trend 'to combine, coordinate or integrate' general, technical and vocational education, 'due to technological progress, increased knowledge and its rapid renewal, which requires more general education for the individual'. Skinner (1978) notes that the tendency to extend general education is not absent from higher education, given developments like the Diploma in Higher Education (Dip HE):

> A determined push from the DES to influence the secondary school away from early specialisation may well result in a more broadly based curriculum and a less academically specialised sixth form . . . Recent changes on the higher education scene would seem to be in line with the movement towards a broader, less specialised curriculum, not only in the sixth form, but in higher education itself.

It is clear, though, that formulating guidelines for nothing more ambitious than closer cooperation between the multitude of useful departures, local variations and confusing anomalies in the tertiary sector is not an easy task. And it can be argued that its very variety is a virtue. The 1979 White Paper seems to take this view:

> The loosely knit framework of departments and agencies is a source of great strength in enabling advances to be made in different ways and at different times in response to specific needs.

But this sounds more like an attempt to justify the *status quo* than a fresh look at a complex problem. More thoughtful support for a loose texture of agencies comes from Briggs (1978):

> We are not yet ready . . . to substitute universal services for independent initiatives. Systematisation can be bureaucratic . . . What we need during the next few years is not imposed pattern, but greater awareness and supported experiment.

Briggs is looking here at the whole field of post-compulsory education, but his argument can be seen as a case for maintaining, and even extending, the diversity of tertiary provision.

We are now in a position to look at the tertiary sector as a whole, and identify unifying issues which run through it from A-level courses at one end to job-oriented skill courses at the other. This question of diversity is a good place to start, since the successful post-war growth of the FE sector owes a great deal to its talent for a quick response to *ad hoc* needs. And the sheer variety of tertiary institutions, viewed simply as a capital asset, means that a crudely imposed pattern makes no economic sense. Furthermore, the students do not readily fall into types; we recognise, for instance, that non-academic sixth formers cannot usefully be called 'new sixth formers', a popular term in the late sixties for those rather coyly described by the 1959 Crowther Report as 'sixth formers with a difference'. There is, as Schools Council *Working Paper 45* (1972) put it, 'a continuum of ability in the sixth form'. As Richard Pring points out in Chapter 2, students cannot be sensibly lumped into two categories.

Forms of tertiary provision, then, must be flexible enough to make use of different institutions and meet different needs. But it does not follow that the search for common structuring devices should be abandoned. The notion of a continuum is double-edged; it calls for variety, but it also implies a certain unity. We are, in effect, saying that, despite their varying interests and talents, 16–19 students face common problems and share common qualities. Can we reconcile freedom of student choice with common educational elements?

For the 11–16 curriculum we can answer in the affirmative. By shifting the notion of choice from choice between different subjects, as in conventional option schemes, to choice within subject areas, as in a common curriculum aimed at mediating the key aspects of the culture for all pupils, we can ensure that each pupil secures a differentiated curriculum within an integrated scheme. Thus two principles which appear to be in conflict can be made mutually reinforcing.

The OECD study *Beyond Compulsory Schooling* recognises that the same principles govern attempts to reform the tertiary sector. But the greater variety of experience students bring into the sector, of institutional processes available within it, and of career aspirations students take out of it, means that the principles can be used to justify very different concepts. The Swedish *Gymnasieskola*, or integrated secondary school, for example, brings under one roof students previously separated in academic and vocational schools, but offers twenty-two alternative curricula in three common cores which retain the same vertical separation. A Norwegian model combines vertical separation with some common horizontal courses in general subjects for all students. And some Canadian and American initiatives (Ontario, Quebec, Parkway School in Philadelphia) have used a system of credits and modules to provide differentiation from a range of basic courses.

These developments help to place in perspective similar English developments which will be examined in later chapters. The tertiary college offers vertically-structured integration, in the main; but the foundation courses of the Open University, and the foundation-year courses at Keele University, offer horizontal integration. The modular structure of BEC and TEC courses provides the same facility. In the English sixth form, general studies is sometimes seen as a way of offering all students a common, horizontally integrated course, and may even bring both first and second year students together for at least part of the programme. In the comprehensive school, as often in university courses, horizontal integration is usually the result of inter-disciplinary links. Thus an 11–16 humanities course for all students might offer experiences using, say, English, history, geography and religious education as contributory subjects and examined output components at GCE/CSE, but providing intrinsic differentiation through the organisation of the learning (Holt 1978).

So in any quest for more unity in the tertiary sector, key issues will be the way integrating elements can be used to offer intrinsic variety and student differentiation. And the case for such a quest rests on three considerations. There is, first, the social and cultural argument for recognising the identity of interest shared by 16–19 year olds. The detailed study by King, Moor and Mundy (1975), for example, looked at 'upper-secondary' education in England, France, West Germany, Italy and Sweden, and gave them 'an intense conviction of the urgent need to *re-think in new terms* the whole teaching/learning/research relationship at the "young adult" level in the

post-compulsory phase of education'. Second, unstructured choice gener-
ates a degree of incoherence which baffles students, and defies the best
efforts of counselling and guidance services, let alone the rather inadequate
provision made in many schools. Consider, for example, the fact that nearly
one-third of traditional sixth-formers get only one A-level pass, or none. It
is clear that many pupils with above-average ability but of a kind not
appreciated by the A-level examiners are taking the wrong course, and
possibly in the wrong place. And we are talking about a small segment of the
age-group entirely in full-time education, and therefore enjoying free
access to whatever guidance is going. The misdirections of other 16–19
students must be legion. The White Paper's 'loosely knit framework' looks
more like a sweepstake than an orderly system.

Third, there are the economic arguments. In the short run this is a
question of avoiding duplication and making the best use of resources. On
top of GCE, CSE, CEE, Royal Society of Arts (RSA) and some City and
Guilds courses in schools, we have OND, BEC and TEC, many City and
Guilds and RSA courses in colleges, along with local courses and new
courses funded by the MSC or the Training Service Agencies:

> The same courses can be taught under different conditions and regulations;
> teachers with the same programmes can be on different pay scales. There are
> different allowances and award systems for different student groups, or for the
> same group in different places (Benn 1978).

In the medium term, the decisive arguments for better coordination are
likely to come from the consequences of a declining school population. After
1982, numbers in the tertiary sector will fall, and the case for all those small
school sixth forms will be extremely vulnerable. This means not only closer
cooperation between schools, and a greater emphasis on separate tertiary
institutions in some areas. It also raises questions about the educational scope
of the comprehensive school. Does it need to have a sixth form? If so, is it
under a doctrinal obligation to provide worthwhile courses for all entering
it? Again, some rationalisation of resources is an inescapable factor.

Underlying issues

In the long term, the economic and educational arguments for coordinating
tertiary programmes and policies merge if we begin to take seriously the
likely consequences of advances in microprocessors and their applications.
Even if we don't, we are bound to see a shift in the labour force from the
productive to the service industries, and an increasing emphasis on
continuing education as the key to re-training and job mobility. If we accept
some of the predicted effects of micro-technology, then we shall move quite
soon into a post-industrial society where there are nothing like enough jobs

to go round; where the few create the wealth of the many; where the Puritan ethic which carried us through the first industrial revolution must give way to the enforced leisure of the second.

This may sound too apocalyptic for some, who recall the dire predictions made in the fifties about the likely effects of automation. But many are taking microprocessors very seriously indeed. In any event, the logic of an advanced technological society is an extended period of general education, and the advent of widespread leisure opportunities gives an extra twist to the argument. We are therefore led back to fundamental questions about the interrelation, in tertiary education, between depth and breadth. Should tertiary courses be less specialised to allow a wider field of study? And what should be the relation between breadth of study and the specialising interest?

These questions have dogged attempts at A-level reform, and no satisfactory resolution is at hand. But they will not go away. They have been much less evident in the FE sector, although the general-education component of many FE courses has been noted, and the 1960s saw a marked growth in liberal studies departments. It is likely that the breadth/depth argument will, in the future, be increasingly in evidence in the whole of the tertiary sector. And this at once challenges the binary structure which is such a marked feature of our English arrangements; the self-justifying distinctions between education and training, between the academic and the vocational. It is difficult to see any difference in scope or intent between a sixth-former taking three A-levels and a sound general studies programme with a degree course and a good job in mind, and an FE student taking a BEC Diploma course and proceeding, for the same reason, to an advanced course and a career in business. In both cases, a regard for learning will be tempered by respect for personal interest and success. And we can draw the same parallel between the one-year sixth former taking a group of O-levels or CEEs, and the college student on a hairdressing course which would include aspects of art and design, communication skills and business administration among others.

While it is one thing to sort out these underlying common questions in the tertiary sector, difficult philosophical dilemmas arise in answering them. We must acknowledge, too, that the attendant issues go beyond education to other social and political matters. Courses, for example, lead to examinations, and public concern with examination standards has emerged in the late seventies as a significant influence on curriculum change. We may regret this, but we cannot ignore it. Another difficulty is that the tertiary sector crosses the boundary between Departments of State. While the DES controls schools and colleges, the Department of Employment runs the MSC and similar enterprises, and the Department of Health and Social Security is responsible for supplementary benefits. Any attempt to clear up the absurdity of some students receiving grants for tertiary courses, while others fend for themselves, raises the issue of maintenance allowances and the value set by the government on education and its contribution to our economic future. This leads at once to the matter of continuous versus continuing education; ought we to 'bring the entire 16 to 18 age group under *educational* guidance' (Simon 1978), or spread the available funds across the whole post-compulsory sector? Should we copy the decision in Norway to give everyone the right to three years of study after the end of compulsory schooling, or introduce, as have other countries, provision for loans and leave of absence? Or can we continue to do nothing much?

We have seen, too, that the funding of tertiary courses can lead to conflict between central government, the local authority and industry. And any significant shift of focus in a craft or technician course from specialist skills to general education would sharpen up these disputes. An attempt to develop a decent day-release system would bring them into the open. It would also raise wider issues to do with the scope and scale of industrial training. Is this simply a matter for resolution between the employers and the trade unions, or does it involve the economic well-being of the country, and therefore justify a measure of public intervention? Is tertiary education simply a matter of pursuing one's academic interests, or learning more about the job one has or aspires to? Or is it also a matter of developing some kind of broader perspective on life, on what our culture has to offer and the shape it might have in the future? It is clear, from our brief look at the general-education element in a variety of tertiary courses and in both schools and colleges, that depth is usually seen in the context of some sort of breadth. But exactly what sort? And where do we stop?

For example, one of the reasons given by the National Association of Teachers in Further and Higher Education (NATFHE) for rejecting the Schools Council's N and F proposals (*Education*, 4.5.79) is their breadth: for 'many of the students in FE take specific courses with very precise objectives—topping up existing qualifications . . . and so on'. The subject basis of A-level is seen as an advantage, compared with requirements for a wider field of study. And some might doubt the enthusiasm of less academic students for craft courses involving compulsory general education. But the success some schools and colleges have had with the CGLI Foundation Course materials suggests much depends on how it is done. At any rate, it is clear yet again that new course and examination structures must combine breadth with considerable flexibility.

Flexibility will be needed, too, in working out the relation between apprenticeships and any extension of so-called education-based systems combining study and work. Trade union attitudes are critical here. An OECD report *Policies for Apprenticeship* (1979) points to a growing desire to develop apprenticeships which impart 'broad, transferable skills'. In England, about one school-leaver in five takes up an apprenticeship; in Germany the figure is about one in two. And while we have 21 per cent of the age-group in full-time general and vocational education, the Germans have 48 per cent. The scale of this disparity is striking, and it applies, too, to the academic end of the range. For while about 15 per cent of our 18 year olds get at least one A-level, the proportion on an academic course in countries like France, Sweden and the US is much higher—between 30 and 80 per cent. It is a curious irony that our efforts to promote curriculum change in the tertiary sector have largely been concentrated on the A-level examination, which concerns so few tertiary students but which we seem to regard as the key to the whole problem. The failure of this approach suggests that the key may lie elsewhere.

Our provision for tertiary education gives no cause for complacency. We need more of it, and it needs to be better organised. But the complexity of the task, and the numerous powerful interests involved inside and outside the government, mean that only a body with the authority of a Royal Commission, and wide terms of reference to match, could do the job effectively. Our Victorian ancestors made good use of this device, as we have seen; but successive post-war governments have fought shy of such a step. It is particularly sad that the 1974 Labour administration failed to establish such an inquiry, given growing concern about existing 16–19 provision, the cool reception given to the Schools Council's proposals for A-level reform, and the development of influential new technology which could profoundly affect social and working life. The danger is that yet again, we shall do too little, too late.

This book cannot undertake to look at the whole sweep of tertiary education in detail. Its focus is full-time education in schools and colleges, and in particular the present and future problems likely to be experienced by schools. But it attempts to look at current provision, and suggest some possible lines of development, in the wider context of tertiary education. Most studies of the 16–19 curriculum in schools have been rather parochial in flavour, and are the poorer for it. It is hoped that in setting the sixth form in this wider perspective, some fresh lines of development can be uncovered.

2

General Education and the 16–19 Sector

RICHARD PRING

I shall in this chapter raise what I believe to be several critical issues in the curriculum provision for the 16–19 sector. First, these issues need to be seen within a particular organisational and social framework, for what is taught and how it is taught are closely bound up with where it is taught, and with the abilities and motivation of those who demand to be taught.

Secondly, I shall give a brief sketch of what is often called 'the traditional sixth-form', indicating some of the strains in maintaining this tradition in the present context. Thirdly, I shall describe the non-traditional sixth-form, showing the kind of curriculum problem that this gives rise to. All this will no doubt be familiar territory to most readers, but important territory none the less to traverse if we are to identify the significant questions about curriculum development. Hence, in the fourth and fifth parts of the chapter I shall formulate what I think are the right questions and then identify key issues that need to be explored if these questions are to be answered.

Context

There are three features of the context which seem central to identifying and sorting out key curriculum questions—the currently expanding market in the 16–19 sector, the development of different organisational frameworks to meet this market, and the proliferation of courses and examinations within each framework.

Let us take the expanding market first. This, as we all know, is the product of both 'the bulge' and 'the trend'. The bulge concerns simply the increase in the 16 year old age group so that, even in terms of present day sixth form traditions, this sector will be making increased demands upon provision. This of course need not in itself force curriculum re-thinking. Things could remain in shape and content much as they are, only there would be more of it (and, of course, expansion in numbers could mean a greater likelihood of things staying as they are, since formerly unviable groups such as 2 or 3 studying Latin for A-level would then become viable). But bulges precede slumps, and the contraction in the total number of 16 year olds between 1977–8 and 1990–1 will be in the region of 25 per cent. (It will be much more in some areas, such as London.) Such a drastic reduction in overall numbers will make necessary quite radical organisational changes. It is doubtful whether many schools will be able to 'go it alone' with viable and balanced sixth forms. It would be totally uneconomic to have several institutions within the same area (let us say, an 11 to 18 comprehensive school and an FE College) competing for the same diminishing number of pupils. I suspect there will be an acceleration of the present trend towards sixth-form centres, sixth-form colleges, and tertiary colleges. The curriculum consequences of such a trend could be quite considerable for we would be moving into a quite different tradition of working.

Hence the first question that I suggest one needs to face is: what curriculum changes will be necessary for 16 to 19 year olds in my school or college as a result of the drastic fall in the relevant age group?

Apart from the bulge there is of course the trend. And by that I mean the trend to remain in full-time education amongst those who in no way aspire to university or indeed any higher education. Such a trend has, of course, been exacerbated by widescale unemployment amongst school leavers. Since this may well be a permanent feature of our economy and our society, the curriculum problems that it gives rise to cannot be met by mere contingency plans. New courses are demanded, and indeed many schools and colleges have responded energetically to provide them. But immediate responses (and those indeed are all that many institutions have had time for) are often unsatisfactory. They are not made against a thorough reappraisal of what the sixth-form education should aim at and how limited resources should be re-allocated. Such reappraisal is necessary when the thinking that previously informed the sixth form belongs to a quite different tradition from the one that would be adequate for a much more heterogeneous set of sixth formers.

Hence, the second question is: in what ways, significant for curriculum decisions, has the traditional sixth form changed in the last 10 years, especially with regard to the ability of the entrants, and their aspirations at the end of their schooling?

The second contextual feature that we must bear in mind is the differentiated scene in which the 16 to 19 sector is now being educated. Not long ago a fairly clear distinction could be made between the academic sixth former, who could aspire to higher education and who would therefore be studying for A-levels, and the practically minded person who, if he were to study full-time, would take a more vocationally-oriented course in a College of Further Education.. Of course, the pattern was never as neat as that. There have always been O and A-level courses in Colleges of Further Education, and sixth-forms have often taken in students who intended to leave at 17. Now, however, it is less and less easy to draw even crude divisions. Firstly, the kinds of organisation offering courses for the 16–19 sector are many: apart from the ordinary sixth form, there are sixth-form centres, sixth-form colleges, technical and art colleges, cooperative arrangements between schools and colleges of further education, and tertiary colleges. There is choice as there has never been before, and the traditional sixth former can now very often opt to move into another kind of institution. There is competition between institutions for a limited market, and the competition is partly between curriculum proposals. Second, some of the newer institutions can offer a wider and more innovatory curriculum than can the traditional sixth form. In a college of further education there are resources that do not exist in schools. Furthermore there is a tradition of immediate relevance to career that is not quite so prevalent in the traditional sixth form. 'Relevance' is a seductive word and we must examine it closely. At the moment I simply wish to point out that the offer of more relevant courses at non-school institutions must to many seem very attractive. The search for relevance must affect the curriculum of these institutions and indirectly the curriculum of the sixth form.

Hence, our third question is: to what extent must the growth of alternative educational institutions for the 16–19 sector affect the shape and content of the sixth-form curriculum?

The third contextual element that we should bear in mind is the proliferation of courses and examinations within the 16–19 sector. Apart from the traditional A-levels, we have:

(a) 'conversion courses' which take students from CSE to O-level, usually in the same subjects;

(b) 'retake courses' which enable the poorly qualified to retake failed O-levels;

(c) CEE which takes pupils in school to a level above their CSE studies;

(d) CFE (the Certificate of Further Education) which allows the same target group to follow a broad-based course with a technical bias;

(e) Foundation Courses of the City and Guilds of London Institute which, also broad-based, aim to help students make a more informed approach to careers;

(f) COS (the Certificate of Office Studies), which is an introduction to commerce;

(g) 'mixed economy' courses which involve both general education (such as study for O-levels) and studies geared to employment;

(h) 'bridging courses' which link the final year at school to a subsequent year at college;

(i)   'occupational selection' and 'which job?' courses, which link assessment for employment with general and remedial education.

The significance in pointing these out is that this is a rapidly growing area affecting schools as well as colleges. There has, for example, been a considerable interest from schools in the City and Guilds Foundation Course. The main reason for the popularity lies in the nice balance between vocational appeal and general education—appealing to the career and practical motivation of pupils without either limiting their horizons or sacrificing to specific training the ideal of general education. Similarly we may note the growing popularity of the Certificate of Office Studies both in colleges and in schools. Their popularity lies in the apparent relevance to the practical ambitions of the students whilst at the same time harnessing to the specific vocational interest more general areas of study. Such a concern for vocation interests of the student tallies of course with the findings of the Schools Council Sixth-form Survey (1970) which gave as an important motivation in the majority of sixth-formers some apparent relevance to practical needs, especially the choice of and preparation for a job. The question (our fourth) that this gives rise to is: to what extent should the appeal to relevance enter into our considerations about appropriate curricula for the 16–19 sector?

To conclude this section, I have pointed out three features of the 16–19 context which affect the curriculum—its expansion both in absolute numbers and in range of aspirations and abilities, to be followed very likely by a contraction of overall numbers; the differentiation of institutions providing for this sector; and finally the proliferation of courses and qualifications aimed at this ever more diverse sector. Each of these features must have curriculum implications—the re-allocation of resources consequent upon the rapid expansion and then equally rapid contraction of numbers, the different educational traditions of school and further education in which the age group can be catered for, and increasing importance attached to relevance in the development of courses. I have tried to capture these curriculum implications in the four questions I have asked. But clearly there is a need, in answering these questions, to get at more fundamental curriculum principles about aims, relevance, structure and content.

The traditional sixth form

I have spoken of different traditions within which curriculum decisions are made. Clearly one such tradition is that of the sixth-form of a school in which the academically more able study a relatively few subjects with a view to gaining entry to higher education. I use the phrase 'the traditional sixth form' because that seems to be both the generally acceptable as well as officially endorsed one. The Crowther Report (1959) picks out the following features of the traditional sixth-form curriculum. It is specialist —that is, the subjects of serious intellectual study are confined to two or three. 'They are interlocking, especially on the science side, and are chosen, at least for potential university candidates, with an eye on faculty requirements.' As the report points out, the remainder of the time (referred to as minority time) is divided between a range of extra studies and activities that generally do not get the full attention of the students. Such specialisation, argues the report, is tied up with educating an elite, an intellectual aristocracy on whom the most stringent academic demands can be made and in whom there can be awakened a real love of learning. It treats them as adults capable of a reverence for knowledge, beginners in a life long quest for truth, which they can share with those who teach them.

The Crowther Report endorsed this principle of specialised and intensive study for the sixth former, who was of course identified with the more able pupil who had one eye on the University. 'Subject-mindedness' it says 'is one of the marks of the sixth-former', and by the time the sixth form is reached concentration upon a limited range of subjects will encourage the study in depth with all the associated qualities of mind that such study engenders. An important characteristic of such in depth and specialised study is its coherence and its integration. Where this is lacking (as, for instance, in a rather unrelated collection of arts subjects), steps should be taken to re-assess the structure and content of the subjects and to look for ways in which one subject might be related to another.

The one criticism that the Crowther Report levelled against such specialisation was that it often left the arts students innumerate and the science student not quite literate. Such imbalance could be rectified by a judicious use of minority time—what it referred to as a complementary element in the curriculum.

This is the tradition of the sixth form that we have inherited. No longer, of course, is it an accurate picture of most sixth forms which are open to a much wider range of abilities and of aspirations. None the less, we may feel that we can distinguish within the sixth form between those to whom this traditional conception of the curriculum does apply and those to whom it doesn't—and to that extent the tradition lives on and influences our curriculum thinking.

Of course, there are external factors too that help to maintain this way of thinking. The demands of university entrance must affect what is practicable and it is clear from recent university criticism of the Schools Council's N and F proposals that it will be difficult to change this concentration in depth upon a narrow range of subjects.

However, the curriculum question remains. Can we identify amongst the expanding 16 to 19 sector a group of people for whom the intensive study in depth of a narrow range of subjects is the most appropriate curriculum?

There are several factors that militate against this conception of the 16 to 19 curriculum. Firstly, the social principles that have re-shaped our school organisation will inevitably re-shape the sixth forms. Such social principles are dominated by the idea of equality. This is a notoriously ambiguous notion, but at least two strands might be detected in the egalitarianism that has re-shaped our educational ideas. There is first the proclaimed right of everyone to continue with their education irrespective of ability or of attainment. Hence, sixth forms have become open to all and are no longer the privileged homes of the academically able. There is secondly the suspicion of hierarchy amongst courses and thus the suspicion of any fostering of an elite group of students taking courses which in some way are regarded as superior to less academic, more practical courses. I am not necessarily agreeing with these egalitarian ideals. In fact, I believe they are often very confused. But they remain a fact of life that influences for better or for worse the composition and structure of the sixth form, and thus indirectly the values placed upon different subjects and activities that compete for limited resources and for a place in the curriculum.

The second factor that militates against the traditional conception of the sixth form curriculum is that, even amongst the select few who were allowed to enter it, a substantial minority was not suited to it. Although it had one eye on university requirements the proportion that actually entered university was surprisingly small.

Thirdly, the criticisms against early specialisation have increased. These arguments are well known and there is no need for me to go into detail. Roughly they are, firstly, that such early specialisation forces a student into a particular career channel long before he or she has the maturity or experience to make an informed decision; and, secondly, that it creates an unbalanced education before students are sufficiently in command of the different realms of meaning or forms of understanding. Lacking in general education, the student will have an unbalanced view of life. There have, of course, been attempts to compensate for this lack of balance—the particular uses of minority time suggested by the Crowther Report, the use of general studies, etc. Bus such tinkerings have not, according to the critics, provided the balance to the specialist emphasis.

From this account of the traditional sixth form and from the criticisms of it, two major questions arise. Firstly, is it possible, in the open sixth forms that now characterise many schools, to identify a viable group of pupils that fits neatly into the conception of sixth form work as described by Crowther? Or are the boundaries between the academic and specialist on the one hand

and the more practical and career-orientated on the other so blurred that one must think more in terms of a continuum from the more able and disinterested searchers after truth to the less academic and pragmatic searcher for immediate material gain? Secondly, where do we stand in relation to the arguments for and against specialisation? Certainly the fashion is to decry it and there are few, except certain sections of the universities, that now publicly argue for it. But are we certain that it should be decried? To answer these questions we need to tackle at greater length the issues of balance, of general education, of the significance of depth, and this I shall introduce later.

The new sixth form?

Again I use a phrase that is common currency. What it usually means is that in the last few years the sixth form, or the equivalent in other institutions, has opened its doors quite liberally to students who would not be aspiring to university or indeed any form of higher education.

There are of course dangers in this way of talking. As I have pointed out the traditional sixth form contained many students who either did not intend to proceed to higher education or ought not to have so intended. Furthermore the so-called new sixth includes a wide range of students in terms both of the purposes for continuing to study full-time and of the abilities and attainments they possess. Hence, I have indicated the need to think not so much of two distinct groups of students within the 16–19 sector but rather of a continuum from those who are capable of academic and disinterested study to those who may be barely literate and who are there simply because there is nowhere else to go. In between is a very large group that is motivated by the possibility of improving career or job prospects, and that is demanding from the curriculum a clear relevance to what is motivating them.

This group will, unlike the traditional sixth form, have relatively low entry qualifications—mainly CSEs grades 2 to 4 with possibly one or two O-levels. They will be looking for courses that have a strong practical content with fairly specific training that will stand them in good stead when they are seeking a job.

The curriculum questions that this group poses are: to what extent should the practical and career seeking motivation of the students enter into the structure and content of courses? Further, to what extent does this concern for relevance to career and for practical training militate against the idea of a continuation into the 16–19 sector of general education?

I have pointed out the difficulties in dividing the 16–19 sector into two distinct categories. Boundaries are too indefinite for that and there are other, just as important, distinctions to be made. A more refined classification might be as follows.

(i) *Academic and pointing to HE (higher education)*
Those who want, and are capable of, a course geared to higher education that is academically demanding and unrewarded by practical relevance.

(ii) *Academic but relevant and pointing to HE*
Those who want, and are capable of, a course geared to higher education that is academically demanding but which is practically relevant, possibly already pointing to practical career patterns such as engineering or medicine or teaching.

(iii) *Conversion and remedial*
Those who want to add to or repeat the O-level or indeed the CSE level examinations already taken. This is a kind of remedial group within the traditional mould.

(iv) *Vocationally relevant, not pointing to HE*
Those who are not motivated by the traditional sixth form pattern of distinct subject centred courses but require relatively short (say, one-year) courses that are at least coherent if not integrated and that are seen to be practically relevant to a vocational interest or indeed commitment.

(v) *Vocationally exploratory*
Those who, like the above students, seek a one year fairly practical course but who have no clear vocational commitments and who require help in finding such a commitment as well as a continuation of their general education.

(vi) *Residual*
Those who are there because they have nowhere else to go or who feel too insecure or incapable to seek a job—the unemployed, the disadvantaged, the handicapped.

It is with the final three groups that I am here chiefly concerned.

Given the wide range of courses and of qualifications now on offer for students in these last three categories, how can schools begin to find their way around? Without some criteria whereby to judge the relevance and value of the courses it is of course impossible. I would suggest the following criteria:

(a) what qualifications, personal qualities, and abilities do these courses demand on entry?

(b) what qualifications and attainments do the courses lead to?

(c) what vocational or career element do the courses contain?
(d) what curriculum content do they require?
(e) what form of teaching or learning do they demand?

An example may help us to grasp the application of these criteria. Following the raising of the school leaving age to 16, the City and Guilds of London Institute consulted a number of schools and colleges in 1973 to determine what, if anything, it could do for 'the new sixth former'. After a series of feasibility and pilot studies, the CGLI made available for 1976–7 and thereafter its foundation courses, aimed at helping young people with the transition from full-time education into the world of work. The courses are based on a study of related groups of occupational and industrial activities, with all the learning having an occupational focus. The motivational importance of success in what one is doing as well as of practical relevance to what one *wants* to do is built in to the course design. In many cases, because of the difficulty of adequate resources important links have been established within the course between school, college, and local industry. One further interesting feature of these courses is that they have begun to erode the previously well defined distinction between fifth and sixth form since some pupils are commencing these courses in the final year of their compulsory schooling.

How would we describe these courses when we apply our criteria?

(a) Entry qualifications: students of about average ability (desirably, several CSEs in the grades 2 to 4) together with some commitment to this or that occupational course.

(b) Exit attainments: a formal certificate giving a detailed profile based on continuous assessment and examination. The level is pre-apprenticeship, but provides a more informed basis for mature choice of further education or employment.

(c) Vocational element: the courses are focused upon industrial and occupational interests, although they aim to educate through such interests, not to train students for them. The industrial and occupational focus of these courses are:

community care	food industries
engineering	art and design
commercial studies	technology
science industries	distribution
public and recreational services	nursing and allied occupations

(d) Curriculum context: six main components relating to a broad occupational focus and providing, altogether, a balanced course of education.

   (i) Industrial and environmental studies—dealing with the structure of the industry, etc, and its place in society and in the environment.
  (ii) Skills and practices—introducing relevant practical skills associated with the occupational focus.
 (iii) Technology, theory and science—connected with the occupational focus.
 (iv) Communication studies—appropriate written, oral, graphical, non-verbal, and numeracy modes of communication.
  (v) Optional activities—not related to the occupational focus.
 (vi) Careers education.

(e) Forms of teaching: practice based and occupation oriented.

Curriculum questions

From what I have so far said it is surely clear that there is a need for a radical re-appraisal of the curriculum for the 16–19 sector. There are different kinds of students for whom there is no traditional set of courses. Those courses that have been traditionally offered are being challenged for various reasons, in particular for the intense specialisation they require. Involved in such criticism and in the search for curriculum solutions are issues of generality versus specialisation, of education versus training, of balance, of relevancy, of breadth versus depth, and of integration versus subjects. Any curriculum review must surely tackle these issues. In the next section I shall briefly indicate the paths along which I believe such an exploration should go. But before that it is necessary to set out the broad questions that need to be answered in any systematic examination of the 16–19 curriculum.

(a) *Whom are we teaching?*

     Any answer to this question would require the identification of distinct groups in so far as these distinctions are (arguably) relevant to curriculum decisions. I have already indicated six groups. The criteria for so classifying students were roughly two: firstly their ability or attainments upon entering the 16–19 sector and secondly their aspirations (whether to improve their career prospects, to enter into higher education, or to escape unemployment).

(b) *What are we aiming to achieve?*

     Statements of aim need to be treated with some caution. Very often they are but the after thought added to one's curriculum planning to make it look rational. I personally do not believe that curriculum planning must begin with completely clear aims. Like anything else curriculum planning often begins with rather vague ideas that become clearer only by trying to put them into practice. Curriculum development must include a good deal of trial and error, and only *gradually* becoming clear about possibilities and worthwhile purposes. None the less, one must begin with certain general orientations, general aims if you like, even if one (quite rightly) refuses to translate these into precise objectives or even if these general orientations are transformed in their very pursuit.

In stating aims one needs to distinguish those which are extrinsic to the learning and education process itself from those which enter into the very definition or account of that process. For example the aim of Bloggs doing history A-level might be, in the extrinsic sense, to get to the university; on the other hand, the aim of engaging in the activity of history (what, as it were, must enter into the definition of this as a purposeful activity) would refer to the development of certain forms of understanding.

Hence, in developing the curriculum for the 16–19 sector, one would need to ask of the different categories of students: why do they want to pursue these studies full-time? Is it to enter higher education, or to prepare themselves more adequately for a job, or to gain a basic literacy, or to gain greater personal maturity and self-confidence, or to postpone choice of jobs until one is better informed?

(c) *What are we teaching?*

Given the overall purpose governing the different courses, one would need to ask about the relevant curriculum content for such aims. For instance, if a substantial group of students aims as in the CGLI foundation course at a better preparation for engineering work—better prepared in terms of a wider grasp of the possibilities, of a mastery of basic skills and understandings, and of the capacity to communicate— then one needs to select that content which introduces students to different kinds of engineering—electronic, mechanical, etc. Further- more, having selected in fairly general terms the curriculum content one would need to reflect upon the nature of this content—its structure, if you like, or how one might characterise the activities picked out by this or that content. For example, for a group of students aiming, in a one year full-time course, at better preparation for office work, one might select as relevant content elementary accounting. But one would in structuring that content for purposes of instruction, also need to think about the purpose of accounting—if you like, the aims intrinsic to the activity, without an understanding of which the activity must seem so arbitrary and meaningless.

What is required here in curriculum development is what I would call philosophical reflection—that is, the reflection upon the nature and structure of that which is to be learnt—the logical structure of the subject matter. For unless one is clear about one's subject or that which one intends to teach, it is difficult to see how one can plan and structure one's teaching, or put into proper sequence the various steps in learning, or show the interrelation of various facts, or produce a syllabus that makes sense to one's colleagues and to one's pupils, or eventually evaluate the success or otherwise of the learner.

It is here too, of course, that questions will arise about the educational value and balance of what is being taught. One must always hold in reserve those more fundamental questions about the general qualities of mind being developed—or, indeed, possibly stunted by too narrow a focus upon the practical and the relevant.

(d) *How should we teach?*

It would be important in the light of what we know about the capabilities and motivation of students in the respective groups to have some view about the relative balance between instruction and self-directed study, or of the need to relate theory to practice or of the need to show the practical (indeed job) relevance of what is being taught.

For instance, ought there not, for certain students, to be much more consideration given to work experience and, at a much lower level, to the sort of sandwich courses and institutional cooperation that were such a fine feature of successful courses in higher education (particularly the Diploma in Technology)?

(e) *How should we organise what we teach?*

The traditional sixth-form curriculum is very much subject-based. One selects, let us say, three subjects from a range of 15 to 20. Often they may be chosen in order to provide a coherent group—let us say, mathematics, physics and chemistry, or Greek, Latin and ancient history. Such apparent coherence is not always easily achieved—as when, for instance, one combines a modern language with history and English literature. But even when there is apparent coherence, each subject will very likely be taught separately without much reference to the others.

Much of the reappraisal of the sixth-form curriculum has been *within* the framework set by the different subjects. After all, the different subject titles are rather loose names covering a fairly undefined set of activities—witness, for example, English or geography. Obvious instances of this reappraisal within the subject at the sixth form level are the Nuffield reforms of A-level syllabuses, in physics, chemistry and biology. But similar reappraisals are currently taking place in the Schools Council Geography 16–19 project, to take into account developments in and changing conceptions of the subject.

But to meet many of the new demands upon the 16–19 sector one may need to think outside purely subject terms in a more integrated way. Instead of thinking of students attending different courses within different subject areas it may be more appropriate to think in terms of a single course integrating different parts. This seems to me to be a crucial distinction. It is the distinction between an education consisting in a group of subject courses *and* an education consisting in a course that integrates a number of subjects.

The distinction between subject based courses and an integrated course is not a clear one, mainly because the word integration covers a wide range of possible organisational arrangements. However, the important question is: what is to be the integrating element? Is it the relevance to a future job, or vocational interest? Is it a major subject for which other subjects provide relevant skills, understandings, information and are therefore subordinate to it? Is it a theme that needs to be explored from different disciplinary angles? Is it a certain core of studies from which spring a variety of options?

(f) *What resources are required (and available)?*

Ideally one should decide what ought to be taught and then ensure one has the resources to teach it. But few of us work in an ideal world and courses need to be tailored to the resources available—the qualifications of the teaching staff and the equipment and space that one can put at the staff's disposal. Hence, as part of the curriculum planning, whether for putting on traditional sixth form courses or for establishing new one year courses, it would be useful to list (i) the staff available—their qualifications and relevant experience, (ii) the available accommodation and equipment, and (iii) whatever local support, such as local industry and commerce, might be approached.

Let us again take an example of how these six questions might be applied to our own curriculum development. A school has an open sixth form of about 150 pupils, many of whom do not and could not aspire to higher education. In asking 'whom are we teaching?' one might well identify one group of 16 year olds of average ability that is unready yet for employment. Either the students are not sure exactly what to do or, having got a fairly good idea, do not feel qualified to pursue it. A large section of such a group might vaguely aspire to some sort of office and clerical work.

The second question then becomes relevant: 'What should we aim to achieve with such a group?' There would possibly be several closely related aims such as to raise standards of literacy and numeracy, to make entry into this kind of employment possible, and to help the students to discriminate more intelligently within the type of employment or between this and other (non clerical) types of employment. Perhaps such aims, if achieved, might be formally certified in, say, the Certificate of Office Studies.

The third question 'what should we teach?' provokes reflection upon the skills, understanding, personal qualities, and knowledge required for this sort of occupation, and (after reflection) some analysis of these different kinds of knowledge, understanding, skills and qualities. It would doubtless require some analysis of skills in carrying out clerical duties (filing, keeping records), abilities in oral and written communication, knowledge about and understanding of commerce and business procedures, appreciation of data presentation, an elementary mastery of book-keeping, some grasp of the law and the legal system, possibly an understanding of social studies and social relations, practical typewriting skills, etc.

The fourth question, concerning how we should teach, raises quite fundamental questions about the relation of theoretical knowledge to practical know-how. In this particular case one would expect an initial emphasis upon this knowing-how, acquired through practical office and clerical work, which gives a basis for subsequent reflection and instruction.

The fifth question concerns the mode of curriculum organisation. The Certificate of Office Studies distinguishes between compulsory core subjects, integrated around the common element of clerical and office practice, and elective subjects which relate to the core in different ways. The new Business Education Council General Diploma (see Chapter 7) similarly distinguishes between core modules and option modules. The improvement of literacy and numeracy are explicitly built into the core modules.

Finally, the answer to the sixth question about resources will depend so much upon the answers to the others, especially question three about methods of teaching. For instance, a more practice-based teaching requires office facilities, though not necessarily within the school or college. Part of the resource review would survey the opportunities provided by the wider community in which the school finds itself. To what extent can local businesses be seen as resources for learning?

Curriculum issues

In what I have said, and especially in those sections concerned with curriculum planning, certain issues have arisen again and again, that require much closer consideration. I list but three:

(a) the relation between education and practical training;

(b) the apparent incompatibility between breadth of coverage and depth of study;

(c) the related problem of a balanced curriculum.

There are of course others, such as integration of courses, that I have touched on but which I cannot develop further here. I shall briefly look at each of these, attempting to show what the issues are.

Education and training
There is often seen to be some opposition between these two terms. Education is concerned with developing desirable qualities of the mind and requires, amongst other things, a fairly broad perspective characterised by knowledge and understanding. Training on the other hand is a preparation for something specific, and often implies little more than the acquisition of a limited range of fairly low level skills. Perhaps in many clerical jobs what is acquired is the well trained office worker who is not well educated—it would be awkward if he were to ask intelligent questions about what he is doing. To be educated is to have transformed in some way one's more general view of life and one's general capacity to act. To be too narrowly trained might provide a limited and limiting vision and an ill-informed commitment to one form of life. Training seems to indicate a narrowness of development that is incompatible with *educational* improvement.

In much that I have said I may seem open to this sort of criticism. I have stressed again and again the practical and the relevance to practice for a large number of sixth formers—in keeping with the importance attached by *them* to vocational relevance.

However, although I would object to any curriculum that was *simply* one of training, I do not see why a training, even in fairly practical and career-orientated activities, cannot at the same time be educational. What makes a training programme educational is *how* it is taught—whether the focus upon specific goals and the acquisition of specific skills are used to raise wider, critical questions and to expand horizons. The course in office studies *could* be a mind-closing operation—limiting the vision of the student, preventing the deeper questioning, shutting out the wider theoretical issues. Or it could be the entrée into these wider issues and the means whereby deeper, more critical questions are raised. Such matters as personnel management could be narrowly focused upon, concentrated upon the specific and the superficial. They could on the other hand be the beginnings of a deeper, even more theoretical, grasp of the quality and nature of social relations and interaction that provides that wider perspective that we normally pick out by the concept of education.

My main point here is then that the contrast should not be between education and training, but between narrow and educative approaches to the training programme. One can be trained to be a doctor in the sense of having one's vision narrowed, and of becoming a skilled but unquestioning and uncritical practitioner. Or one can be educated through one's training to be a doctor. It depends on how one teaches rather than upon what one teaches. Thus the City and Guilds Foundation Courses aim to educate *through* training and *through* vocational interest, and not to train for that vocational interest as a rather poor substitute for education. Hence the problem is, not that of choosing between education and training, but of training in such a way that the specific focus will raise wider educational questions. Typewriting by itself is hardly educative. Learning skills of office work, when these are set in the broader context of commerce, social relations and problems of communication, can be.

The question is then: how might more general educational interests and more general qualities of mind be harnessed to practical concerns and particular training programmes?

Breadth and depth
Although specialist emphasis to the exclusion of breadth was endorsed by the Crowther Report, it has constantly been attacked. Roughly the argument is that 16-plus is too early to complete the development on a broad front that should characterise the educated man. The well-trained scientist, who has an inadequate grasp of language and who lacks the sensibility developed through the humanities, would not be regarded as educated.

The philosophical backing to this sort of argument is roughly of the following kind. Education is concerned with the development of knowledge and understanding. Knowledge and understanding are of different kinds. To acquire knowledge and understanding of one or of a few kinds only is to get a distorted view of reality—not seeing things as they should be seen. Hence, the educated man should be familiar with all the different kinds of knowledge. Without such general education, the specific, in-depth studies will doubtless produce a clever person (scientist, historian or whatever) but not an educated one, who sees the limitations of any particular discipline or any particular perspective.

Clearly the philosophical writing relevant to this particular view point is that of such educational thinkers as Hirst (1965) and Phenix (1964). These two have taken a God-like view of the whole domain of knowledge and understanding, and have divided it into seven or eight fundamental kinds. A general education would draw upon all these kinds of knowledge.

We see this philosophical position reflected in Schools Council *Working Paper 45: Growth and Response* (1972). There an attempt is made to pick out the elements in a balanced curriculum, and then, for purposes of the sixth form curriculum, to equate these with traditional subject areas. The elements are eight in number: literacy, numeracy, knowledge of physical environment, knowledge of social environment, moral sensibility, aesthetic sensibility, fashioning the environment (creative arts, etc), physical education.

I am not impressed with this approach. Firstly, for reasons that I cannot go into here, it depends too much upon a particular philosophical position that is itself questionable—namely, that the domain of human understanding can thus be divided into 6 realms of meaning or 7 forms of knowledge or 8 elements. Secondly, it is likely to lead to a continued disintegration of the curriculum into the bits and pieces, which will be dealt with very superficially.

A different way of achieving breadth, that we have seen in some of the courses already referred to in this chapter, is to broaden the perspective within which 'focused' studies are to be seen. The Dainton Report (1968), concerned with the swing away from maths and science in the sixth forms, spoke of humanising these courses. Thus A-level courses in science could be devised in which the philosophical, historical, and social aspects of science could become part of the course. I have always thought that one way of understanding science as an activity is through the historical development of scientific ideas. Yet how rarely does one see courses in the history and philosophy of science in the sixth form—as part of the science package.

But this, of course, is far from the only way of getting at general education through the particular. One worry I have about the model proposed in *Working Paper 45* is that each of these elements is seen as a logically discrete category. But clearly this is not the case. Literacy and numeracy are modes of understanding and of operating upon the world that permeate all other activities. Just as we are now used to calls to 'language across the curriculum' lower down the school, so we might develop a policy of language and numeracy across the curriculum in the sixth form. It would be a matter not of having a literacy element in order to produce a balanced curriculum but of stressing a greater degree of literacy in the approach to the specialised studies.

Hence, far from seeing breadth and depth as two separate positions in the education or training dichotomy, rather do I suggest that one tries to broaden the perspective within which the narrow focus is placed. And this can be done at any level from that of the one-year pre-apprenticeship course to A-level.

Balance

Problems about 'balance' are really part of the issues raised above. But maybe we could begin to tackle these issues by asking what we mean when we talk about a balanced curriculum. Let me make a few suggestions of what it could mean. There can be balance:

(a) between different kinds of knowledge (what *Working Paper 45* had in mind);
(b) between content, skills, attitudes (between being theoretical and being practical);
(c) between what is done within school and what is done outside;
(d) between different teaching styles (e.g. discussing, lecturing, work-centred etc);
(e) between different kinds of interesting and motivating activities.

Which notion of balance has one in mind? What appears balanced to the 'consumer' (pupil or parent) may not appear so to the provider (the teacher or curriculum developer). Questions of balance therefore depend on the point of view—and the educational philosophy behind that point of view. Roughly there seem to prevail two kinds of educational philosophy in this matter: that which clings to a notion of general education put forward by *Working Paper 45* and thus of balance between the different kinds of knowledge. And that which centres upon the needs of the sixth former, providing balance from that point of view and endeavouring to broaden the perspective within which that point of view is sustained. And it is the latter that I am more and more convinced is the right way forward, whether in the development of A-level courses or (as with CGLI foundation courses) in the one-year post-16 full-time course.

3
Curriculum Breadth and Examination Reform

The last major change in the English sixth form took place nearly thirty years ago, when the old Higher School Certificate (HSC) gave way to what was conceived as a two-level examination—the General Certificate of Education at Advanced and Scholarship levels. Since 1951 there have been profound changes in society and the structure of our education system, and an expansion in all areas of knowledge. These have been reflected in the way the 11–16 secondary curriculum is organised and taught, and in the structure and examination procedures of many university courses. Comprehensive schools have appeared on the one hand, and new kinds of higher education institutions on the other. There are new courses and new qualifications both before the sixth form, and after it: but not in the sixth form itself. All that has happened—or almost all—is that GCE S-level has virtually vanished, and GCE A-level holds sovereign sway. The potential university entrant of 1980 operates within precisely the same framework of curriculum and examinations as he did in 1951. For eighty per cent of the time he will concentrate on examination work, and he can narrow his focus just as remorselessly on, say, English, French and History in this era of desk-top computers and hypermarkets as he did in the years of post-war austerity and four-figure log tables. If anything, the competition for university places will make him even more wary of irrelevant diversions; what matters is not just three A levels, but good grades as well. In 1951 he could aim for Oxbridge, and still take a part in HMS Pinafore; now it could turn a certain A grade into a shaky B, and spoil his chances. The grip of A-level is tighter than ever.

This is a remarkable state of affairs, because its grip extends beyond the university candidate to all those who take two-year courses, and even to some one-year sixth formers. It is perhaps difficult for us, who have lived through and worked in the unchanging sixth form for so long, to stand outside it and recognise how relentlessly the A-level examination determines the curriculum for most sixth formers. Yet, as Judge (1974) has written,

> To ask for the movement of a frontier or for a shift in perspective, is to ask only that some of the principles which apply unchallenged to curricula in higher

education should apply also to those for the sixth form. A university would be amused rather than offended if it were required to relate the study pattern of each of its members to some common curricular model . . .

It doesn't seem too much to ask, and the question has been posed ever since the Crowther Report in 1959 endorsed 'the English principle of specialisation, or intensive study, as it would be better described'. Headmasters, the Standing Conference on University Entrance and Schools Council working parties are unanimous in urging less sixth form specialisation, and a broader curriculum: scarcely had the Crowther ink dried, when Peterson (1960) led the attack on its bland assumptions that 'specialisation is a mark of the Sixth Form, and "subject-mindedness" of the Sixth Former'. And since its first meeting in 1964, the Schools Council has struggled to secure agreement on a more broadly based sixth-form programme. Yet its current proposals are open to important objections, and in any event could not, in the Council's view, be implemented before 1984. It is clear, if nothing else, that the A-level exam and the specialised framework it predicates give rise to deep, reinforcing resonances in the English sixth form. Change can only come about if these are identified and resolved.

The grammar-school influence

Let us look first at some historical and political factors. Taylor, Reid and Holley (1974) have observed that:

> In almost all major respects the foundations on which education in the sixth form was raised, and on which it has continued to operate throughout this century, were Victorian. No basic change has yet taken place in these foundations of the sixth form and its curriculum; they have merely become obscured, while their effect on the lower forms of the school has consolidated their own position.

In their admirable study, they trace the notion of the specialised curriculum from its invention by Samuel Butler, while headmaster of Shrewsbury school from 1798 to 1836, to its universal adoption by the Victorian public schools; so that when the Balfour Act of 1902 led to the expansion of day grammar schools, it seemed inevitable that they should model their sixth forms on those of the public schools, then perhaps at their apogee of esteem and influence. In that way they would hope to give able pupils what Cyril Norwood, for 25 years the chairman of the Secondary Schools Examination Council, called 'the best possible chance of winning open scholarships . . . the rare and refreshing fruit that the schools hope to gather' (quoted in Edwards, 1970). Butler's innovation was to stress intellectual performance, and to use examinations not as a test of teaching efficiency, but as a meritocratic device to promote competition and select the fittest. This need not, in itself, imply a specialised curriculum. But at that time classics had no competitors, and Butler's methods gave the universities a string of classical scholars. The backwash effect meant that when other subjects were later introduced, they tended to be organised into 'sides' so as to occupy, like classics, the whole of the curriculum. Thus the science side appeared in the latter half of the century, and in due course the 'modern' side with English, history or modern languages.

The growth of this pattern owed much to the distinctive position in nineteenth century education of the public schools as virtually the only vehicles for academic preferment, and to the great power wielded by their headmasters. The pattern helped the universities of Oxford and Cambridge to postpone reform, and the close connexions between the two systems are still in evidence. Even so, it did not pass unchallenged, and figures of the eminence of Dean Farrar and Matthew Arnold were aware that on the continent, government intervention had led to a quite different pattern, now evident in the broad curriculum of the German *Abitur* and the French *Baccalaureate*. They urged that both literary and scientific elements should be part of the pre-university course, and by the 1870s these arguments had gathered much support. But, as Taylor, Reid and Holley put it,

> Perhaps if the state had intervened at this stage it would have been on the side of the integrated curriculum throughout the secondary school. The fact is that the climate of opinion never again seemed so propitious to the integrated curriculum.

So it came about that the grammar school, between the wars, settled down to a mid-Victorian curriculum which was efficiently serviced by the Higher School Certificate. The HSC had been introduced in 1917, and was based on 'a more concentrated study of a connected group of subjects'. Passes were awarded in two principal subjects with two subsidiary subjects, or three principal and one subsidiary; but the universities preferred the latter pattern and it generally prevailed. The principal subjects were to be drawn from a prescribed group, which was at first either classical studies, mathematics and science, or modern studies. Other subjects were added in the 1930s, but until 1937 the regulations forbade the combination of an arts principal subject with one from the science side. And by then the habit of specialisation had become imprinted on the schools' consciousness. Post-war growth in grammar-school sixth forms did little to change the pattern; in the late 1940s, combinations of arts and science subjects were still rare.

By this time, the connexion in teachers' minds between specialised sixth-form study and true learning was probably as much emotional as rational. 'It stimulated interest, maintained high standards of work, kept teachers close to university methods and material and added to their status' (Edwards 1970). But the HSC had two functions: one was certainly to provide for entry to higher education, but the other was to serve as a higher leaving certificate, to be 'a suitable test of two years' work for the average pupil'. As competition mounted, first for university awards and then even for university places, the schools turned it into a better instrument for the first function, but a worse instrument for the second. The Norwood Committee's first suggestion for resolving this inherent problem was an Intermediate Certificate, at a standard somewhere between the School Certificate, taken at 15 or 16, and the Higher Certificate. At this point the reader may well experience a sensation of *déjà vu*: there is little new in the interminable arguments about the sixth form, and the same ideas seem to recur in a cyclic fashion. This particular proposal pleased the girls' schools, who had many one-year sixth formers bound for nursing or commerce, and who had grown restless under the yoke of HSC: but it pleased few others. It was argued that the lower standard of exam would promote less intensive study, would push up the standards of the higher exam, and place a further burden on hard-pressed schools. These arguments have, of course, a not unfamiliar ring about them.

So the final Norwood solution, which eventually became GCE A and S-levels, was different, but essentially on the same two-tier lines. The two functions were separated, and the hope was that S-level would be used for potential university scholars, leaving A-level to act as a measure of satisfactory course completion. But the GCE had two further aims. The first was to introduce more continuity over the whole 11–18 curriculum, and the second was to provide more flexibility in the sixth form. It was argued that, since an O-level pass could be awarded on A-level papers, and an A-level on S-level papers, then a pupil could take subjects at three different levels in the same year, and in particular could by-pass O-level in the subjects he proposed to pursue in the sixth. It was, indeed, explicitly stated that 'It would be contrary to the intentions of the system for any pupil to sit successfully for two or three levels in the same subject'. The idea was that a pupil's course need not be tied to fixed exam hurdles, and could be planned as a whole, matching the work to the teacher's assessment of his ability and achievement. But teachers are reluctant to trust their own judgment, and if an exam exists they tend to use it. So O-level was used exactly like School Certificate, and A-level much like the HSC principal subjects.

But there was scope for flexibility, because the requirement that subjects should fall into prescribed groups, as for the School and Higher Certificate, was dropped. Instead, all three levels of the GCE were single-subject examinations, with no requirement for either grouping or coherent courses. The way was now open for schools to allow combinations between subjects that would reflect the pupil's interests and talents, and the same principle was adopted when the CSE examination was introduced in the 1960s. The Schools Council for curriculum and examinations took over most of the functions of the old Secondary Schools Examinations Council, and has clung to its faith in the single subject examination. Its affirmation of this, as the basis for any reformed sixth-form examination system, has imposed an important constraint on the solutions which successive working parties have devised. But while the notion of the grouped or structured examination seems to be unacceptable in schools, it is widely used in further education. It is the principle on which the highly successful National Diploma Courses are run, and continues in their BEC and TEC replacements.

The dominance of A-level

There can be little argument that the grouping of School and Higher Certificate was rigid and confining, and there is no case for a return to anything as crude and restrictive. The single-subject basis of O-level and CSE allowed comprehensive schools to make schooling work across the ability range by arranging multiple option schemes in the fourth and fifth years. But in effect the examination system is still determining the curriculum; because of the exam structure, a range of subject-based courses can take the place of coherent curriculum planning. School Certificate did at least ensure that the curriculum covered certain areas of study. What is at fault is not so much the idea of the single-subject exam, but rather its existence in a characteristically English kind of curriculum vacuum. In the absence of any set of guidelines, or even clear educational objectives, it is inevitable that market forces, and whatever is familiar and convenient, will determine how the empty space is to be filled. It is only very recently, with the growth of curriculum studies on the one hand and of disenchantment with the cafeteria-based curriculum on the other, that public opinion and that of the Inspectorate have moved towards the idea of a unified, coherent curriculum. And the practical experience of schools using this approach shows that it can be adequately served by the O-level/CSE single-subject system.

In the sixth form, it was the very adaptability conferred on A-level by its single subject basis which enabled it to flourish. The HSC had already prepared the ground, and S-level fell into desuetude as the two-year three-A-level course settled in for a long innings. And although arts/science mixes were now theoretically possible, the Crowther Committee of 1959 was sure enough of its ground to be able to assert 'subject-mindedness' almost as a psychological fact—and by subjects it meant science and mathematics, or the humanities. Peterson, in the following year, produced evidence that many more sixth formers would have preferred a combination of arts and

science subjects than were able to do so, and similar inclinations emerged
from the Schools Council survey of 1970. Yet King, Moor and Mundy (1975)
suggest that little has changed in many sixth forms:

> In one academically successful school in our sample, which prides itself on the
> broad range of available subjects, and where over 90 per cent of the students . . .
> were doing three or more A-levels, almost 43 per cent were taking those
> examinations entirely in mathematics and physics . . . Even within the range of
> choices, the variation is predominantly confined to the most familiar options.

Market forces are doing their work at 18-plus, just as they have at 16-plus.
Schools are keen to sell their top-of-the-range product—students who
perform well at conventional examinations—to the universities who are
only too eager, as a rule, to take them. The two-year three-A-level course
has thus become the straitjacket for the sixth form curriculum, finely tuned
for university entrance but patently unsatisfactory as a higher leaving
certificate. The need for reform is as evident today as it was to the Norwood
Committee of 1943. We are better off, in that arts/science combinations are
freely permissible; but in some ways worse off, in that the subsidiary subject
has disappeared. Undoubtedly one reason for the decline in modern
languages, for instance, is that the HSC allowed the maths and science
student to take subsidiary French or German, and many did; the three A-
level pattern leaves no time for such frills, except perhaps as re-take O-
levels in the first year, which is not by any means the same thing.

We have looked at some of the factors for the pre-eminence of A-level,
and can now recognise that perhaps the most important of all is its ability to
respond to the changing demands made on the sixth form curriculum, and
yet go on basically unchanged. For teachers, it is familiar and reasonably
predictable, and therefore easy and convenient to teach to a satisfactory
level. The marking loads are considerable, and the imaginative teacher will
always be looking for a new response to the challenge of his subject and his
new students. But for many, the A-level course offers an annual opportunity
to shake hands with an old friend. And for schools, it's a real windfall that an
examination originally intended for the top 15–20 per cent of the ability
range can be made to work, more or less, for an altogether larger slice. A-
level is almost a kind of universal wall plug which fits so many oddly-shaped
holes, and on which a variety of courses can be hung. Since the average size
of an A-level class is only 8, any more differentiated exam system would
spread the available teaching capacity more thinly and reduce class sizes still
further. By extending the number of A-levels offered from the basic 8 or 9 to
12 or 14, the small comprehensive school can ostensibly meet the needs of all
its two-year sixth formers at moderate cost in teaching time and negligible

effort in curriculum planning. Little wonder that the A-level citadel has proved so impregnable.

Before we go on to look at attempts to change all this, it is worth pausing to ask how it really came about that a system devised a century and a half ago in a public school on the Welsh marches should have become so deeply entrenched. The key political events are, I think, those of the 1940s. The fact that the 1944 Education Act makes no mention of either curriculum or examinations is one of its marvels, and possibly one of its strengths. The GCE reforms of 1947–1951 are equally well intentioned. But the combination of these two events meant that control of the curriculum slipped away, and the concept of teacher autonomy took its place. Teacher autonomy without curriculum planning is a *laissez-faire* recipe, and post-war expansion did nothing to diminish the powerful forces that had already shaped a specialised curriculum. The rest follows.

Attempts at reform

In some ways, the post-war history of the attempts to change matters is less interesting than that of the preceding period. The same arguments and suggestions look stale when they come round for the second and third time. Criticism of the traditional sixth form curriculum can be set under three headings: first, dissatisfaction with the curriculum for educational reasons; second, dissatisfaction with examinations for practical reasons; and third, attacks based on economic factors. Arguments that the curriculum should be broader, or show balance, or introduce more choice, come under the first heading. Under the second come attacks on A-level as an examination, and on the absence of an alternative to O-level for one-year sixth formers. The third is a more recent arrival, and has taken two forms. One is based on the proposition that because our economic prosperity depends on technological advance, mathematics and science should be continuing elements in the sixth form programme; the other unpretentiously asserts that an average sixth-form set of only 8 wastes valuable resources, and it focuses on the organisational factors which could give more efficient working.

If we look first at the educational arguments, we must note that the effect of A-level in promoting specialisation, without the compensating effect of subsidiary subjects, had become evident by the mid-1950s. By the time the Crowther Committee met at the end of this decade, many schools offered non-examined courses which eventually became known as general studies. But Crowther noted that most of the courses were more anxious to make science specialists literate, than introduce arts specialists to a background knowledge of maths and science. In the category of *complementary* courses, the committee placed those courses designed to compensate the scientist for his supposed ignorance of the arts, and vice versa; while *common* courses presented material which was supposed to be of general benefit to all students, and might include physical and religious education, music, philosophy and head-magisterial pep-talks. Crowther backed the idea of the specialised A-level curriculum, but wanted also to see more weight given to these minority-time studies.

The central difficulty was, and is, that the main purpose of sixth-form life is to do well in the A-level exams; it matters as much to staff as to students. So devoting teacher effort to the preparation of courses which students are inclined to see as irrelevant to the main task may seem somewhat unappealing. Even so, in 1961 a group of public and grammar schools signed an 'Agreement to Broaden the Curriculum', which pledged the 'ABC' schools to devote at least a third of the sixth-form timetable to general studies of both common and complementary kinds. Another provision was to prevent specialisation in arts or sciences before the sixth year; for the backwash effect of A-level had been to extend premature specialisation down even to the third year in the lower forms. But a Schools Council Research Study of 1973 found that choices were still being made as early as this, and commented that 'By their choices at that time many young people are effectively closing the options available to them in the sixth form'. It is clear, then, that this and similar initiatives had no real effect.

Yet at the time of its establishment in 1964, hopes were high that the Schools Council, by bringing together representatives of the DES, the LEAs, the universities and the schools, would at last cut the knot and release sixth form students from their thrall. The first fruits of its early resolution to give priority to the study of the sixth form curriculum and examinations appeared as *Working Paper 5* in 1966. This was pretty much a case of HSC rides again, the idea being that a student should take two major subjects, each equivalent to A-level, and two minor. These were two-year courses, and were reckoned to occupy 24 of the 35 periods in the week. Significantly, the remainder were for non-examination work, with at least 6 for general studies. There were no HSC-like restrictions, though, on the choice of subjects, and the hope was that while the university aspirant would use the minors to reinforce the majors, the less academically inclined could be offered a broader course.

The objections to this scheme centred on the problems the small sixth forms in comprehensive schools would encounter in providing so many courses. We have already noted the logistic advantages offered by A-level in this respect. And we must note that whatever the educational rationale behind the proposals, one is bound to describe them in terms of an examination structure. So we have moved from the first set of arguments to the second, because the new proposals, like those before and since, emerged not from a fundamental curriculum analysis, but from an unswerving tendency to see examination reform as synonymous with curriculum reform. Taylor, Reid and Holley (1974) note that *Working Paper 5* urged the Schools Council to undertake a study of 'the historical growth and contemporary relevance' of the concepts implicit in 'specialisation', 'study in depth' and 'general education'. It seems a great pity that this was never commissioned.

In 1967 a modified form of the major and minor scheme appeared, as *Working Paper 16*. The difficulties of the schools were met by allowing them to devise the minor subjects, now called 'electives', from their own resources; and they could be one or two year courses. And presumably to offset the element of novelty involved in this piece of school-based curriculum development, the two major subjects now became two conventional A-levels. But this second shot at a two-tier system failed to appeal to either the schools or the universities. The schools produced a fresh argument: the two A-levels would dominate the curriculum at the expense of the electives, and thus tend to make it more specialised. And the universities mistrusted the element of internal assessment implicit in the electives. Yet potentially this could have been a scheme of real educational merit, if the schools were equipped to do the curriculum planning that it required. Their reaction suggests—and this is surely correct—that they were not. But one can imagine a scheme which would have suggested possible structures for electives around various pairs of A-levels, thus giving both breadth and coherence. The new element of structure would perhaps have met the misgivings of the universities, while reassuring the schools that the electives were within their capacity and had a major supportive role to play. In subsequent curriculum developments—for instance, the Integrated Science Project—the Schools Council were to produce materials which left the schools a good deal of freedom in how they were to put them together, and the General Studies Project is another particularly relevant example. But in the context of a whole new structure for the sixth form, we can conclude that neither the schools nor the council were ready for this departure from the established pattern of research, development and diffusion projects—and it would have smacked a bit of council interference in the schools' curriculum affairs. But again, we must record another lost opportunity.

It is appropriate at this point to remark that the mid-sixties saw another development which resulted from the second kind of dissatisfaction with A-level—with its usefulness as an examination. In 1963 the report of the Robbins Committee on Higher Education noted the increasing reliance placed on A-level as a selective device for university entrance, and recommended research into methods of testing aptitude. 'If some of the predictive load could be shifted from examinations, the pressure upon candidates to cram for them would be less . . .' The committee was plainly exercised by the dual use to which A-level was being put: as a monitor of student performance, and as a predictor of university success. The committee noted that the US made extensive use of Scholastic Aptitude Tests (SATs) for college entrance, and in 1965 the DES and the Schools Council funded a project to develop and evaluate a similar instrument, which became known as the Test of Academic Aptitude (TAA). In the event, after devising and administering the tests to a sample of students, and following them through their university careers, the exercise proved abortive:

> The hopes of high correlation between TAA scores and subsequent academic performance have not been fulfilled. In general, although scores on the aptitude test are positively related to success at university, the correlations are substantially lower than those obtained in similar studies in the United States, and have even less predictive power than GCE A-level grades (Choppin and Orr, 1976).

The main reason for the superior American performance of these devices seems to lie in the fact that while the tests are applied to an unscreened student population in the US, in England and Wales potential university entrants have already passed through the discriminatory sieves of O-level and A-level.

The inadequacy of A-level as a predictive instrument has been shown by a number of research studies. Reviewing them, Choppin and Fara (1972) note the undesirable backwash effect of university entrance requirements on school syllabuses below sixth form level, which

> could perhaps be excused if A levels were really an effective predictor of later performance. But all the research shows that this is not the case . . . A-levels correlate only poorly with subsequent examinations . . . However . . . although A-level results fall a long way short of perfection, they do provide the best single predictor of university success.

Correlation between A-level scores and degree class seems typically to lie around the 0.2 level (Choppin and Orr 1976). So the best that can be done, in making predictions, is to combine A-level with other information, such as O-level results and school reports. The general conclusion we can draw is that the mesh between A-level and university work is far looser than is conventionally assumed. The assertion by the Standing Conference on University Entrance (1978), in its response to the N and F proposals, that 'A-level generally provides a satisfactory grounding for entrants . . . It also appears to discriminate among the most able candidates' is scarcely borne out by the research.

Two other attempts to reform the sixth-form curriculum resulting from the dominance of A-level must be mentioned before we take a look at the Schools Council's N and F scheme. In 1968 a body quite different from the Schools Council—the Council for Scientific Policy—came up with the report of a committee chaired by Professor Dainton and which took a quite different approach. Their concern with sixth-form breadth stemmed from economic rather than educational reasons. The education system is a convenient scapegoat when economic issues become politically important, and the reflex appeared again in 1976 with the launching of the 'great debate'. The Dainton Committee considered that, whatever the educational needs of sixth formers (which were no part of its brief), the needs of a technological society for an adequate flow of scientists and technologists into universities would be met only if every sixth former took mathematics, along with a further three or four subjects spread across science, social science and the arts. It was remarkable that a committee charged with the task of taking a strictly instrumental view of sixth-form education should be led to conclude that the solution lay in 'the wider objective of meeting the needs of the individual pupils for a rounded education'. Scientists and technologists, the Dainton Report recognised, must be

> articulate and literate . . . They must be aware of, and sensitive to, the boundary areas where their activity is felt: economic, social, humanitarian, organisational, governmental. The longer their early studies can keep open this breadth of approach, the better.

The Dainton Report perceived that particular sixth-form problems could be resolved only in the context of its curriculum and the aims of sixth-form education. In contrast, the Schools Council's suggestions up to this point give the impression that tinkering with the examination structure is all that is needed.

In the same year (1964) in which the Dainton Report was published, the Headmasters' Association threw its hat in the ring with a document, 'The Sixth Form of the Future', which inclined more to coherence than breadth as an objective to pursue. Its unduly harsh comments on the Dainton Report bear this out:

> Here again we encounter rigidity and inflexibility: the idea of a curriculum pattern into which all sixth-formers are to be fitted, regardless of their various needs . . . The advantages of study in depth for those pupils who are ready to commit themselves to such an approach are to be discarded.

The headmasters' view of study in depth would involve the specialist 'in reaching out in a number of directions from his own centre of interest, broadening his vision, his understanding, his perception of relationships, his sympathies and compassion'. They were surely right to recognise that the student's own interests are the vital focus, and that aspects of a general education must be integrally related to that focus in a meaningful way. But their specific proposals were an unhappy mixture: one primary subject could be taken with one or two secondary subjects, with the primary including a broadening general paper, and with intermediate level courses also available. It is difficult to reconcile this imposing array of courses with their objections to *Working Paper 16*.

In 1969, the Schools Council took a double-barrelled shotgun to the problem: one barrel was a new Joint Working Party which linked the council with the Standing Committee on University Entrance, and the other was a reloaded Sixth Form Working Party. They came up conjointly with a variant on the two-tier scheme: five subjects after one year, and three after two years, with the first five chosen from a grouping scheme which thus made a reappearance after having sunk with HSC in 1951. It proved a popular target for the objectors, but most of their fire was reserved for the rather fatuous suggestion that two of the five subjects should be examined after one year, and the other three after two years; making, with O-level/CSE, three exams in three consecutive years. By this time the saga of the sixth form was beginning to look more like a farce, with the unfortunate difference that the script was by the Schools Council rather than Ben Travers, and therefore much less entertaining.

The N and F scheme emerges

The council now ordered its Working Parties to do their homework again, and in 1972 the Second Sixth Form Working Party published *Working Paper 45* as the first part of its report. This was a workmanlike affair and had a good reception. The new aim was to be 'a balanced curriculum', and was supported by an analysis which would have benefited from a philosophical contribution. But at last, curriculum issues were brought to the surface, and it was accepted that balance could be achieved in different ways: 'The answers may lead us to a traditional, subject-based curriculum, or they may not'. But in fact, they did: balance was to result chiefly from allocating five-sevenths of a pupil's time to five main subjects, which might represent a spread across the 'elements of a balanced curriculum'. On the other hand, they might not: no grouping method was suggested this time round. The remaining 30 per cent of the timetable was to be minority time, where a curious distinction was drawn between general education and general studies, while both were to contribute to the balance of the whole curriculum. Current affairs, careers, art, music and games count as general education, but religion, logic and philosophy are general studies. It looks as if philosophy is more important than art, or at any rate recreational rather than formal. This is probably not the intention, but in general the paper's handling of epistemological questions is its weakest part. It is, however, indicated that once the right pattern of balance is established in the five main subjects, the general studies component should be integratory rather than compensatory. A team-teaching approach is suggested, which confirms that, in Crowther terminology, common rather than complementary courses are in mind here.

In the following year this working party produced its proposals for the examination structure as *Working Paper 46*, and the Joint Working Party produced a discussion paper as *Working Paper 47*. The final recommend-ation which emerged from all this was that two-year students should take five subjects at 'Normal' or N-level, each subject requiring about half the study time of an A-level; and that degree aspirants could be examined at a 'Further' or F-level, requiring about three-quarters the study time of an A-level. *Working Paper 47* declared that no university course requirements 'should demand more than two subjects at the Further level. We see some advantage . . . if departments could limit their named further subject demands to one—or none.'

The response to N and F

Despite the considerable exertions of the Schools Council to show that its proposals were desirable and practicable, they failed to gain a wide basis of support and in March 1979, the Labour Secretary for Education (Mrs Williams) stated that the Government was not committed to the abolition of A-levels. In the following month the retention of A-levels was urged by the Head Masters' Conference, the National Association of Head Teachers and leading teachers' organisations. Only the National Union of Teachers remained loyal to the N and F scheme which, through its controlling interest in the Schools Council, it had backed from the beginning. In June the Committee of Vice-Chancellors observed that 'the universities are overwhelmingly of the view that the N and F scheme does not offer an acceptable solution' to the problems arising from the wide range of ability in sixth forms. Within days, the Conservative Secretary for Education (Mr Carlisle) had written to the Schools Council to say that it would be wrong to replace A-levels for the foreseeable future: their standards should be maintained.

No one, however, with a regard for the opportunities lacking in the existing sixth-form curriculum, and the needs of the country and its citizens in the uncertain years that lie ahead, can imagine that A-level plus general studies can continue to prevail into the twenty-first century. The DES has invited the Schools Council to look at the wider introduction of alternative O-levels (AO), as a supplement to A-levels. Although the GCE boards offer a number of AO papers, the fact that they count technically only as O-level standard has made them an unattractive proposition in schools. But this is only picking at the problem, and the DES has declared its intention to conduct a departmental inquiry into the whole 16 to 19 area. Inevitably, therefore, the search for alternatives to A-level will have to be renewed at some point, and it seems worthwhile to look back briefly at the N and F experience and see what can be learnt from it.

In a note of dissent to *Working Paper 47*, Sir Alan Richmond argued that the introduction of F-level and so the creation yet again of a two-tier system was undesirable. And it should be noted that, in the subsequent discussion, the polytechnics at least expressed their readiness to accept 5 N-levels as an entry requirement. It seems impossible, though, to satisfy the university lobby with any broader subject-based curriculum than the three A-level system without introducing a higher tier. Representative university bodies for physics and even English declared that the 3N+2F formula would mean four-year honours degree courses, and the former chairman of the *Working Paper 47* committee suggested that 'medical students could perhaps be expected to cope with three Fs, two Ns. Other variants would be four Fs with one O-level or three Fs, one N and one O-level' (*The Times Educational Supplement*, 24.3.78). Richmond's fears were well justified.

Another difficulty with schemes which advocate new exams based on fractions of A-level is that the laws of arithmetic seem to bend when applied to the division of courses and examinations. Many Open University students, for example, are aware that two half-unit courses involve more work, in the aggregate, than one whole-unit course. This is only to be expected, since getting under the skin of a subject means crossing the threshold of its basic concepts and techniques. With a five-subject curriculum, this has to be done more often than with three A-levels. And if the five are to cover a broad area of the culture, then there is none of the overlap which can arise with standard A-level combinations. Something has to give, and there was always the risk that N and F would make general studies even more of a Cinderella area than at present. *Working Paper 60* (1978) remarked, a touch ominously: 'General studies might still have a place, but in the context of a broadened examined curriculum its place would need to be reassessed'. This leaves the certainties of *Working Paper 45* some way behind.

Another N and F uncertainty was the nature of the link between N and A-level. The function of N-level was twofold: to broaden the curriculum for conventional university-directed A-level students, and to develop syllabuses 'such that a wider range of students than those who find A-level courses satisfactory should benefit from them' (*Working Paper 60*). For although over 80 per cent of students entering the sixth form to take A-levels aim at three or more subjects, nearly a third either fail them or pass only one. Can we assume, then, that N-level will be less hard than A-level? *Working Paper 60* noted that N-level courses would have about half the total study time of an A-level, but added that

> This is not to say that a subject at N-level is in fact based on half of an A-level syllabus; N-level is a new concept *based on the varying needs of the students who will study for its examination.*

Without knowing more about these students, the words I have italicised are merely tautologous. It is clear that the bulk—the extensive property—of N-level is to be half that of A-level. But will it be half as intensive? *Working Paper 60* is again ambiguous. The construction of N-level courses 'is best done by considering N-level as a new concept rather than by scaling down A-level syllabuses'. But we are also told that N-level will provide the basis 'for more advanced study', and that 'in many cases the philosophy behind the courses at N-level is very similar to A-level'. Small wonder that the Mathematics Syllabus Steering Group for N and F concluded that 'We are therefore not able to close this report with an agreed recommendation', and instead listed ten fundamental questions for the next round in this complicated game.

An interesting result of this equivocation about the academic status of N-level was the promotion by various bodies of other combinations than N+F. As the pure milk of N+F began to curdle, the Schools Council rushed out a 'progress report' (1979) listing 14 different examination schemes for the sixth form, based mainly on permutations of A, N and F-levels, and which had each attracted some support. Two of these are of interest here. One is a single-tier solution, which had the support of the Association of University Teachers. The AUT argued that four F-levels would be a satisfactory scheme, and that they could include one arts and one science subject, still leaving 20 per cent unexamined time for 'cultural and social awareness' studies (report in *Education*, 29.12.78). Apart from the expense of N as well as F, 'Higher education and prestige employers would use F-levels predominantly, and N-levels would be disregarded'. This suggests that a four-subject spread is the most the university traffic will bear. But at least the second tier is eliminated, and in so far as F-level was defined as three-quarters of an A-level, the scheme was built around a less demanding examination which might have suited a wider range of students than A-level. Another last-ditch scheme harked back to some of the Schools Council's 1960's proposals, and argued for retaining A-level alongside N-level. The snag with this is that few university entrants would be likely to bother with Ns: they would aim for the hard currency of As.

It is a curious irony that in some ways the effect of the N and F proposals on the debate about the sixth-form examination system has been not to broaden it, but to polarise it. The line between potential university entrants and other two-year students looks firmer than ever. If academic students want breadth, they must take four examined subjects and so work harder for it; *ergo*, we may end up with even fewer of them. The others may have breadth by means of N-level, but cannot expect it to share the academic billing with A-level. In short, a two-tier system seems to imply a two-tier student structure.

One-year courses and examinations

So far we have concentrated, like the would-be reformers, on the problems of two-year students and the remarkable survival power of A-level. We must now turn to the curriculum of one-year sixth-formers. In 1959, the Crowther Report noticed that 'new sixth formers' of varying academic standard 'are found in increasing numbers in comprehensive schools', and numbers continued to grow as staying-on rates improved in the affluent sixties, and more comprehensives sought to build up their sixth forms. Some of these students were re-taking O-levels, possibly prior to starting the A-level course the following year. Others might be filling in time before careers in nursing, or the police force. Some might have no career prospect in mind, insufficient ability to cope with A-level, but like the idea of a year in the sixth. While grammar schools have tended to choke off this one-year growth, comprehensive schools have encouraged it. Heads and staff have, for one thing, sensed a certain educational imperative—to run an open-access policy and offer something for everyone. But a bigger sixth form has other benefits. It brings more staff, more senior posts and more resources; it confers status; and it is a useful bargaining counter in reorganisation schemes.

In 1970 the Schools Council formally recognised that O-level was far from the ideal answer as the mainstay of one-year courses, and resolved that there should be 'some form of extended CSE examination . . . available for older students'. It fell to the lot of the Second Sixth Form Working Party to make a specific proposal, and by this time plans to replace O-level and CSE by a common system of examination at 16-plus, and devise new examinations at 18-plus, were well advanced. The new 17-plus examination had to fit in with these existing commitments, rather than evolve from a study of the curriculum issues and the students' needs. The working party plumped, in *Working Paper 45*, for another single-subject examination, to be called the Certificate of Extended Education, and aimed at one-year sixth-formers with CSE passes at grades 2 to 4. The CEE was seen as the basis for a complete one-year course: 'Planning for the CEE should be on the basis that it would normally be taken in as many as five subjects'. It was hoped, too, that the CEE would produce courses with new content, and also more adventurous teaching methods:

> We ought to be able to offer these young people some alternative to the unexciting prospect of going over very much the same kind of ground as they did a year earlier, whether it be by straight repeats of syllabuses they have been taught already, or by a repetition of conventional fifth-form teaching techniques in another subject.

Several examination boards launched pilot CEE schemes, and a number of schools and colleges adopted the new examination in the expectation that it would gain DES approval, and in particular for the equivalence of CEE grades 1–3 to an O-level pass. In commenting on the CEE proposal, though, the Secretary of State noted that 'a good many teachers and schools think that the CEE target group should be enlarged to include abler pupils than those for whom the Schools Council say the examination is intended', and considered that if this were done it would be 'less useful to the young people who ought to benefit most from it!'. Finally, in 1978, she set up the Keohane Committee to consider CEE 'in relation to other courses and examinations for those for whom the CEE is intended'.

Meanwhile, a study of one-year courses (Vincent and Dean, 1977) has shown just how unsatisfactory a basis O-level is for one-year courses. Although O-level work constituted the main course for over 40 per cent of one-year students, the success rate was low. The average school or college student taking O-levels on a one-year course passed 1.3 O-levels in the fifth year, attempted 4.2 in the sixth, but passed only 1.4 of them. In comprehensives the average number passed after the sixth-form year was only 1.1. In the sample investigated by Vincent and Dean, the average comprehensive sixth form totalled 117, with 72 in the lower sixth. Between 20 and 30 per cent of school lower-sixth students were taking one-year courses, with an average of 27 per cent in comprehensives. Using the full-course criterion of students with 5 or more CSE passes at 16-plus and a mean pass grade between 2 and 4, Vincent and Dean found about half the one-year students would be suitable. If the criterion is broadened to include any students with this mean CSE pass grade, then about 70 per cent of one-year students in comprehensive-school sixth forms would lie in the target group for one or more CEE subjects.

In practice, the relatively small number of schools and colleges using CEE have not necessarily kept strictly to these criteria. For one thing, CEE courses vary between boards. Some offer Mode 1 syllabuses with a highly academic flavour, so that O-level may be a softer option and possibly one that offers the teacher more scope. Others give the school or college a good deal of elbow room. The attraction of CEE for sixth-form colleges is that it can provide a flexible examination strategy, particularly when the considerable resources of the colleges are used to develop new teaching methods and materials. Thus CEE might be used instead of O-level as a 17-plus examination for almost all lower-sixth students—including those on two-year A-level courses. And the strong local reputation of a thriving college can overcome national doubts about its validity.

Some schools, however, have lacked the will or resources to pump life into the CEE; while others have committed themselves to Mode 3 approaches. But in reviewing the CEE, the Standing Committee on University Entrance has augustly commented (1978):

> The Conference notes however that Mode 3 syllabuses and schemes of examining have been a prominent feature of the experimental examinations . . . It considers that the acceptance of the recommended equivalences with CSE and O-level would depend on . . . an adequate scheme for validating the assessments on a national scale.

The problem is that Mode 3 strategies are likely to be most needed with less strongly motivated students. But there is little incentive for schools to make the extra effort if there is doubt about its acceptance. To some extent, DES fears that CEE is moving up the ability range are the result of the lack of a clear DES lead.

And in any case, the lack of suitable one-year post-16 courses is a peculiarity of schools and sixth-form colleges: in further education a great range of courses is available, and it is significant that the take-up of CEE in FE and tertiary colleges is almost non-existent. Free from the limitations of the single-subject examination, FE institutions have evolved course-based programmes centring around some vocational theme. And whereas CEE can cope only with 70 per cent of school one-year students, on Vincent and Dean's estimate (1977), FE courses are plainly adequate for the whole range of students. It is therefore fair to ask whether, after all, CEE is really necessary.

The question is certainly apt in the light of the development, since 1974, of its foundation courses by the City and Guilds of London Institute. In 1978 there were 25,000 subject entries for CEE, compared with about 3,000 course entries for foundation courses. But the CGLI entry is expected to double in 1979 (Doe and Haddock, 1978), maintaining the geometric growth rate of these courses. And a single student entry for a foundation course can be equivalent to five CEE entries. The structure of the foundation courses has been outlined in Chapter 2. They differ from CEE in a number of ways, and fundamentally in that the course fills virtually the whole programme. Assessment is carried out partly by the school and partly by the CGLI, and teachers are involved in a good deal of curriculum development work. Essentially, they must answer the question 'How does the subject matter being taught contribute to the total desired outcomes of the curriculum?' They must therefore look beyond their own subjects to the contributions of others, and possibly beyond their school to other institutions, since the courses lend themselves to cooperation between school and college. The courses may also be taken by fourth and fifth year students, and in a few schools where this is happening one or two CSE subjects—usually maths and English—may be taken as well. But there must be reservations about offering foundation courses with a clear vocational bias to students of this age; in effect, 13 year olds may have to decide on their future career, which puts the clock back to the vocational courses once popular in secondary modern schools. It is equally clear, though, that the introduction of the CGLI courses at this level reflects the failure of multiple-option schemes to engage pupils, particularly those who are poorly motivated or of below average ability.

The City and Guilds Institute has taken pains not to define the target group for its foundation courses too closely: they are 'for young people of about average ability'. But they obviously share at least some common ground with CEE, and in its 1979 report, the Keohane Committee has both endorsed CEE and urged a closer link with FE courses. The success of the foundation courses will depend on how effective they are at getting students jobs, and it is too early to say much about this. But schools which have adopted the courses seem to be satisfied, and while few employers seem to have heard of CEE or even CSE, the City and Guilds Institute enjoys a high reputation for its craftsman and technician courses. Subjective matters of this kind can often be decisive, and the failure of the DES and Schools Council to spend money on a campaign to establish the image of CSE with industrial employers is particularly sad; all the more so because it is now too late.

In 1977 the DES set up the Further Education Curriculum Review and Development Unit (FEU), and its particular concern has been the 16–19 age group. There has been minimal representation from further education on the Schools Council, although it has increased slightly under the 1978 constitution. And *Working Paper 45* broke new ground in devoting a chapter to 'The FE Alternative'. But it had no brief to link the two systems, and had to settle for the usual platitudes about the need for school/college cooperation. So although one ought to welcome the advent of the FEU as a coordinating agency which might eventually help to tidy up part of the 16–19 scene, it has to be regarded as further proof of the DES fixation with binary systems. The existence of the FEU alongside the Schools Council can only make it harder to bring a unified view to bear. But the FEU has published a helpful report (1979) on 'one-year pre-employment courses', which proposes a curriculum framework comprising a common core of 50 to 60 per cent of the course time, with the remainder divided between vocational and job-specific studies. This attempt to rationalise an aspect of 16–19 provision must be welcomed, and the Keohane Committee acknowledge that it reinforced their view that proficiency tests in English and mathematics should be part of CEE. The introduction of this course-based element within a single-subject exam is a significant new departure, as is the other Keohane recommendation that CEE should be a pass/fail exam, with an additional category of 'pass with merit'.

Although the CEE has moved further towards official acceptance, the sixth-form landscape is still as much dominated by GCE O and A-level as when the Crowther Report appeared, twenty years ago. The Schools Council's attempts to replace A-level with a broader pattern of single-subject examinations have led inexorably to two-tier solutions, and without solving the problem of an 18-plus system which can act both as a leaving certificate and as a visa for entry to higher education. As Maclure (1975) has remarked, 'The A-level committees represent old-style pre-Sputnik type curriculum planning—civilised discourse . . . laced with the distillation of practical experience within the present system'.

Curriculum change needs a less complacent approach, and it is the case that the only genuine and immediately available alternatives to sixth-form O and A-levels are the result of private enterprise by autonomous bodies. One of these is the foundation course provision developed by the CGLI: the other is the International Baccalaureate (IB), which Richard Whitfield discusses in the next chapter. This scheme was first conceived by a group of teachers in the International School of Geneva, and quickly took shape after a substantial grant from the Ford Foundation in 1967. The N and F scheme bears a remarkable resemblance to the IB, and it is an interesting irony that the Schools Council is, in 1980, planning a joint IB feasibility study. It should be noted, though, that this project was seen from the beginning as 'an opportunity for experiment and research in curricula and examinations which could have an innovatory effect on national systems' (Peterson, 1972). This emphasis on curriculum considerations seems to have a more dynamic model in mind than that which emerges from *Working Paper 45*. And the International Baccalaureate ensures that its students pursue a broad course by defining subject groupings and making a coherent general studies scheme an integral part of the timetable. Not the least of the lessons to be learnt from the N and F saga is that a prescriptive scheme must be self-consistent. To compromise on the underpinning curriculum issues can be fatal.

4

Subject Structures in a Coherent Curriculum

RICHARD WHITFIELD

This chapter adopts the premiss referred to in Chapter 1, arising from Schools Council *Working Paper 45* (1972), that there is a continuum of academic and other abilities among the 16 to 19 age group who participate in a full-time formal education in whatever kind of institutional structure. I suggest that the curriculum for this age group should pay at least some attention to a common framework of aims for all students built upon the outcomes of preceding stages in the educational system, yet sensitively adapted to individuals' emerging talents, interests and vocational aspirations. Incorporated into the chapter are several key issues of concern to schools in their sixth-form planning, for example problems associated with options, institutional curricular unification, general studies courses and examination structures; the particular example of the International Baccalaureate is referred to in some detail for possible adaptation within a range of British institutions. However, the chapter is fundamentally about curricular aims and complementary outline administrative frameworks which, bearing in mind the nature of the educational system, must be both adapted and extrapolated within individual local contexts.

Introduction

Systematic discussion of the curriculum appropriate to any stage during the formal educational process is contingent upon viewing that process both as a whole and in relation to the contemporary social context in which it is enacted. Curriculum planning for the 16–19 age group must consider both the *preceding* curricular foundations from the pre-school years onwards (but more immediately the 11–16 stage) and the *ensuing* employment and/or tertiary level requirements of students participating at this level. However, in the British context, that is easier said than done because of the diversity of both institutions and ages of transfer and of detailed curricular provision in classroom, workshop and laboratory. Nevertheless the concept of 'curricular balance' continues to be found useful to educational practitioners, even though theorists are far from unanimous as to how the idea should or can be characterised.

Here, albeit briefly, the scene must be set from first principles upon which there would seem little to disagree about among both practitioners and theorists. Let us agree that the central aim of education is to help youngsters to become, through learning, competent, socially responsible, self-directing and fulfilled persons. In so far as the formal curriculum is both perceived as and, in reality, is a crucial medium for the achievement of this overarching aim, it is necessary to unpack the constituents of 'competence', 'social responsibility', 'self-directioning' and 'personal fulfillment' in relation to the wider social and economic scenario in which each individual is developing. That is a formidable task which will forever defeat even the most computerised educational planner. Any educationally worthwhile curriculum must be sensitive to time and place and to the unique characteristics of the actors—both teachers and taught; yet if a truly individualised curriculum is, practically speaking, an impossibility, are there to be no structural guidelines, at whatever stage, which can characterise the educational process as more than a collection of idiosyncratic encounters? It is around the concept of 'balance' that analyses consequent upon a refusal to accept curriculum *laissez-faire* and a view of persons as inhabitants of widely distinct, non-overlapping cultural realities must be centred.

General education: a brief analysis

'General education' has always been a difficult concept to characterise—certainly much more so than the defining of specialised education, or vocational education or skill training. Yet it is with the base of a 'general education' that traditional curricular forms for 16–19 year olds, whether of the specialised academic A/S level type or of a more directly vocational character in further education (for example secretarial and trades courses), have had to build, adding, for almost all students, 'broadening', 'balancing', or 'remedial' elements. Hence discussion of curricular balance for this age group requires the analysis of prior curricular experience.

Modern interpretations of general education in democracies owe much to the classical concept of a 'liberal' education—education for the 'free' man. A sound general education is thus to be associated with assisting youngsters towards individual freedom, towards autonomy, towards a critical yet constructive citizenship. Today, the weight of philosophical opinion suggests that such a general education is centrally concerned with the development of mind in certain distinctive and differentiated modes of human consciousness and experience. These qualities of mind, which involve knowledge, understanding and judgment, can control to a significant degree physical skills and emotional responses, and they underpin the concept of the whole man. General education viewed in these terms places upon the educational system a weighty moral obligation to seek to initiate *all* students into these differentiated modes of human experience, each of which is essential for the mental health, the intellectual and emotional stability of the person. This suggests that there are elements or modes of human consciousness which, like the bodily vitamins, are or can be common among different individuals and even societies; that is, they are potential characteristics of *homo sapiens*.

If this is granted, and there have yet to appear cogent arguments which would undermine these basic principles, it is of paramount importance for the structure of a general education curriculum and the choices within it to determine what these modes of conscious experience might be. This is chiefly a matter of analysis of the nature of human knowledge, understanding and experience, not in a philosophical vaccum, but as it interacts with persons psychologically and set against the socio-historical perspective of man's attempts to make sense out of his world and of the reality of his predicament within it. Work in the theory of knowledge suggests that there are about six differentiated modes of human consciousness. ('About six' will here have to suffice because the precise characterisation of these modes as 'forms of knowledge' or 'realms of meaning' remains an issue for academic debate amongst philosophers which need not centrally concern us here.) The interrelated series of meanings which man has devised to understand the world may be classified as:

(a) *symbolic* meanings—derived from communication systems conforming to internally consistent rule systems, for example: mathematics, languages, symbolic logic and chemical shorthand; these meanings are based upon axiomatic or quasiaxiomatic systems;

(b) *empirical* meanings—based upon concepts whose truth is subject to tests by controlled observation using the senses of instrumental extensions of them, as in the natural sciences;

(c) *aesthetic* meanings—derived from sensory, and in part intuitive, experience set against idealised perceptions of visual, tactile and auditory form;

(d) *relational* meanings—derived from relationships with other people and things, signifying that man's identity is not formed in a vacuum, but in relation to other persons and objects.

(e) *ethical* meanings—based upon moral concepts and codes concerning human thoughts and action; and

(f) *'perspective'* meanings—derived from overarching concepts of time,

place, God, the ultimate reality and so on; these dimensions shape
further aspects of the human identity and can be mediated through
subjects such as history, geography, theology and philosophy.

It may be noted in passing that this list is in many ways similar to the areas
of development specified for monitoring in secondary schools by the DES
Assessment of Performance Unit viz:

  (i) mathematical and linguistic communication,
 (ii) scientific activity,
(iii) aesthetic expression,
(iv) personal and social development,
 (v) physical development,

in which areas of motor coordination (v) seem, at least superficially, an
addition to the list with a merging of areas (d) to (f) under (iv). The six fold
classification is far from arbitrary, and the areas are not as distinct as they
appear, and may be depicted hierarchically by the following diagram.

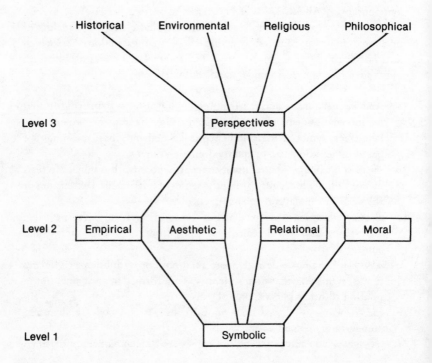

Each mode of understanding is, however, characterised by four criteria which, if taken together, are unique for each domain. These criteria are:

(a) characteristic basic concepts, such as angle, noun, force, beauty, love, duty and so on;

(b) characteristic structures between concepts, such as theorem, sentence, atomic theory, work of art, home, legal code, creed;

(c) characteristic methods of inquiry, for example derivation, experiment, interviewing, surveying and prayer; and

(d) characteristic tests for the meaning or truth of statements and propositions, such as internal consistency, observation, appreciation, valuing and religious experience.

It is in the last of these criteria, the 'truth tests', that there is considerable difficulty in describing the precise character of particularly the last four modes of human understanding described briefly above. Traditional school science for example tended to accentuate criteria (a) and (c) rather than (b) and (d); retrospectively it might be suggested that Nuffield science has tended perhaps to over-redress this balance. Giving this concrete example indicates how the criteria (a) to (d) may be used practically by teachers to test for balance of their classroom activities within a domain.

Within the model being developed here, man, once having satisfied the basic biological necessities for survival of warmth, food and health, is portrayed as a truth-or meaning-seeker, believing life to contain both intelligibility and purpose rather than nonsense and meaninglessness. This view of man is one of hope rather than cynicism, and of events one of order rather than chaos. The 'whole' man in these terms is one able to derive meanings, experience understandings and display skills in each domain, and the motivation to become 'whole' lies in the restless quest for intelligibility. General education on this view has as its central task the successful initiation of youngsters into these modes of awareness so that they can function both autonomously in each, and autonomously as persons. The six areas of meaning which have been described emphasise the public shared consciousness of man as a species. But his private, individual realities, experiences, imaginings, meanings and creations—emphasising the uniqueness of the individual person—need not be obliterated, even though for their personal intelligibility they are at some point related to the more articulate public constructs of reality.

Balancing a general education curriculum

In the light of this analysis, balancing a curriculum for a general education becomes a much more subtle task for the schools than that of ensuring some kind of notional arts/science mix. C. P. Snow's 'two cultures', while appealing to the popular mind, has only a limited message for the structure of the school curriculum and the rubrics which might govern choices within it. A justified general education has more of a six-sided, than two-sided character. The aim is to help pupils towards wholeness through participation of mind, emotion and body in the six differentiated modes of experience. Such an ideal (see, for example, Whitfield 1971) gives the curriculum, and those participating in it, directions, a structure and a coherence. Through it the pupil can have the beginnings of a framework against which to make sense of all that life can involve—at both work and play, in both pleasure and pain, and in the worlds of both theorising and practical living.

However, aims and ideals, if they are to have a reality, must be translated into compatible administrative structures and procedures. The balanced general education to which I have referred may be realised in practice in the schools through the institution of a complementary supra-subject faculty structure. Many medium or large secondary schools have in recent years set up faculty structures, but the number and character of the faculties which are institutionalised are matters of considerable educational concern, for the

A SCHOOL FACULTY STRUCTURE

SCHOOL FACULTY OF	SUB-FACULTY DEPARTMENTS	AREA OF HUMAN MEANING CHIEFLY DEVELOPED
1. Languages	English, French and other foreign languages	*Communications*
2. Mathematics	Faculty as single Department	
3. Natural Sciences	Physics, chemistry, biology and earth sciences	*Empirical enquiry*
4. Creative Studies	Art, crafts (including technical), music, literature and drama	*Aesthetic expression*
5. Human Sciences	Domestic sciences, psychology, sociology, economics, civics, pre-parent and careers education, physical education and outdoor pursuits	*Relationships* (home, local, national and international communities)
6. Humanities	Geography, history (including non-linguistic classical studies), religious studies, moral education	*Moral awareness* and *human perspectives* (temporal, environmental and eternal)

faculties become the most potent power structure, particularly in the senior common room, for determining the balance of the whole curriculum. There is reason to believe that some schools have developed faculty structures, the character of which is difficult to justify.

The table shows *an example* of an interdependent faculty structure for schools which reflects the six areas of human meaning as outlined. The subject department elements within the table are of course familiar. What the structure suggested does is to highlight justifiable relationships between them so that the topology of the curriculum and its resources might be shifted to become compatible to the concept of general education. Such a structure is possible for middle and secondary schools and some compatible examples already exist (see, for example, Holt 1978).

Much more could be said by way of justifying this or a similar structure; it does of course begin to stipulate areas of experience which *any* pupil's general education must not avoid if that pupil is not to be left at the risk of a lopsided or stunted consciousness. Lest the example be misunderstood the following practical points may serve to clarify what is being suggested.

(i) Each faculty, and the departments within it, might be fundamentally concerned with the development of meanings in the respective areas indicated. This does not imply that some subjects, whose logic is presently open to diverse interpretations, could not appear within a major category different from that indicated in the Table. For example, some teachers of literature and drama might prefer to view their work as mainly developing interpersonal and moral understanding rather than aesthetic expression; equally, some teachers of modern educational dance within physical education might adopt a converse justification within the framework of meanings. Other subjects, whose logic is less flexible, for example the natural sciences, could not be moved within the framework without doing an injustice to their essential character. The six areas of meaning thus provide a criterion against which curriculum balance can be checked, and equally important, they act as a filter for rejecting other claimants for curricular time. The faculty structure presupposes that every subject department has articulated its major and minor areas of contribution within the whole to enable sensible planning of both the whole curriculum and its constituent parts to take place. Every teacher on the school staff thus understands both the nature of his own contribution (aims, content and methods) as well as that of other colleagues in the team effort of assisting pupils towards wholeness.

(ii) Physical education, careers guidance, crafts and domestic science, so often left on their own apart from the academic structure of the school, are brought into the core of the enterprise to reflect the cognitive as well as motor-emotional outcomes of these subjects. Physical education for example has an intellectual potential which is so often neglected, and it might through contemplative and self-regulatory techniques be a powerful medium for mind-body equilibration. Pre-parent education might now possibly be ranked as one of the nation's foremost priorities (Whitfield 1979).

(iii) The differentiated, though inter-related, nature of the faculties militates against ill-conceived notions of curriculum integration and topic-based studies. For *inter*-faculty work *interdisciplinary* approaches will be stressed, in which the distinctive logical character of the different disciplines is respected. *Intra*-faculty work may well result in more *integrated* courses of study, such as integrated science. (My distinction in this often confused terminology would permit courses of 'interdisciplinary science' planned by several faculties.)

(iv) A 'special educational services unit' for pupils who lack a threshold competence in the basic skills of reading and writing and understanding of numbers is also likely to be required for some time for pupils up to age 16, but programmes for these children should adopt the same fundamental aim of a differentiated awareness and understanding.

(v) Each faculty for a general education programme up to say age 16 would be accorded the same status, in terms of, for example, staffing and timetable time, since all areas of meaning are at this stage of equal importance. (It is a senseless question to ask if moral education is more important than science education; the two are different aspects of general education—unique yet subtly inter-related.) The Faculty of Science in this framework might thus receive about 15 per cent of the teaching staff and timetable time for girls as well as boys, so that science can become a recognisable component of the curriculum from about the age of 8, and later study not curtailed by administrative procedures which force early specialisation towards languages, the crafts, or to science itself. The 'time-on-task' variable is, not surprisingly, significant in studies of educational outcomes.

(vi) Modifications to the faculty resource allocations just suggested for the 16–19 age group will depend upon the particular styles of specialisation/ partial specialisation adopted; we return to this issue later.

Subject groupings, faculties and choice

The faculties which have been suggested group the myriad of school subjects more or less according to their logical character. No other basis seems readily justifiable from both theoretical and pedagogical viewpoints. These faculties thus provide guidelines for the more rational grouping of subject options. Option groups should be based more upon what taught subjects can deliver without aborting their character, rather than upon essentially non-educational constraints such as present school buildings and staff resources, which over time at least are amenable to change. There is perhaps no more curious aspect of secondary school curricula than the bizarre array of option groupings which are devised, particularly for 14 to 16 year olds, which are poor substitutes for curriculum planning.

By the time a pupil leaves school, or enters a more specialised curriculum (surely never before the age of 15?), we must ensure that he or she has had sufficient contact with and initiation in each of the domains of human experience which, perhaps regrettably, are not left lying around in the 'outside' society, like the air we breathe. This is not possible with a supermarket or 'a la carte' curriculum, with free, unstructured choice for which, paradoxically, there is mounting evidence of its actual restriction of genuine choice (see, for example, DES Survey 21 1975, and Weston 1977). It becomes possible with a 'table d'hote' curriculum containing about six compulsory 'courses', with choice laid on as far as practicable within each 'course'. Whatever options are provided by the different faculties within the school structure, (and for reasons of diversity, richness and motivation, especially for adolescents, a school with no curriculum choice prior to the minimum leaving age would be a barren and unreal place), every pupil must take courses from each faculty, in due proportion over the years at school. This kind of strategy at least up to the age of 16 may prevent the present tendency to replace 'selection by school' by 'selection by curriculum'.

Such a restriction is not as rigid as it may at first seem, for there is no reason why we should regard general education as proceeding by broad quanta of semesters, terms or academic years. Schools generally have their pupils for a minimum of four or five years; for those staying on in the sixth form the period is of course longer by at least one year. Providing we have a strategy and monitoring system for the individual student over the whole period of care (and across institutions if necessary), there is no reason why over relatively short periods as interest, conceptual readiness and learning rate dictate, there should not be biases within students' programmes. While being properly concerned with sequence and progression, we must not bind ourselves blindly to the notion of linearity of study in all subjects. And if we are really concerned about general education, some school time might for all pupils be of a 'remedial' character—improving those areas of under-standing, skill and insight which are deficient; very few pupils are strong in everything. For example, cognitive excellence may be accompanied by motor deficiency. Within faculties a choice, increasing in range as pupils grow older, is envisaged. In the earlier 'foundation' years, each faculty's programme should be rich and diverse so that pupils have a basis for real and responsible participation in choices when they are offered later on. In science, for example, they should all, regardless of sex, have genuine opportunities for physical, chemical, biological, geological and astronomical experience so that later selections and rejections are both real and informed. Similarly, in aesthetic experience they should have opportunities for singing, instrumental playing, dancing, acting, working with paint, wood, metal, plastic and so on; in fact, here there is perhaps the best opportunity for the early exercise of pupils' individual skills and interests set within the contextual and conceptual bounds of aesthetics.

Application to 16–19 age range

We now turn to the significance of the foregoing discussion for the range of students likely to enter our sixth forms or their equivalents in the future. Hitherto, and quite naturally, the relatively small proportion of students capable of or wishing to take A-level type courses has governed most of our thinking in this sphere, which in turn has been dominated by the relatively restricted access of the 18-plus cohort to higher education. However, in whatever arrangements are made in the sixth forms of the future, the nation ignores proper consideration of the intellectually able student at its peril; ways must be found of retaining some of the educational benefits enshrined, albeit for a few, in the A and S-level traditions. Egalitarian idealism must not forever run away from the realities of the specialised academic and professional competencies required of minorities within the modern world, which are in any case crucial for the achievement and maintenance of a dignified life for the majority.

For the 16–19 cohort a curriculum based upon the notion of *limited specialisation*, whether academic or vocational, seems most appropriate. Just as the junior school curriculum tends to become differentiated into components which may be labelled over a period of two or three years as pupils' perceptions of knowledge and activity categories develops, so we should see a perhaps more gradual transition from general to intensively specialised educational programmes. The 16 to 19 years would seem both maturationally and institutionally the most appropriate phase for this latter transition for the majority of students, preparing them more adequately than most existing curricular schemes for the more highly specialised work in higher and further education.

The N and F proposals of the Schools Council (*Working Paper 60* 1978), which are the most recent signpost in the two-decades-old debate on the overspecialised character of the sixth form curriculum, are underpinned by a commitment to limit specialist studies more than heretofore. However they do not unfortunately incorporate rubrics which, arising from analyses of the nature of human knowledge and experience, might guarantee the desired objective. There is no clear analysis of what is to be understood by a 'subject' and any recommendations about the crucial, though difficult issue of subject groupings which might govern and structure student choice are avoided; this could if implemented lead in some cases to greater, rather than less, specialisation, for example a five subject cluster of pure and applied mathematics, statistics, computer science and physics. Market forces are no substitute for policies to achieve widely valued educational aims, and *Working Paper 60* curiously concludes that 'the only circumstances in which some grouping system (of subjects) might be justified would be if it became apparent that students' choices of subjects were not providing them with a broader curriculum.' But in the terms of this chapter, curricular breadth is not necessarily directly related to the number of subjects studied or offered at external examinations.

The transition towards full specialisation at 18+ or 19+ during the sixth form years might be far better viewed as a *differential* time allocation to the six modes of consciousness outlined earlier. Each mode would continue to be studied at least in some measure by all students but with markedly different emphases—of time, content, and teaching strategies—according to students' abilities, motivation and likely career aspirations. Within such a framework a sensitive educational guidance and pastoral care system is assumed, as is a complementary scheme of assessment pitched at about three different levels, not necessarily dissimilar in outline to the CEE/N/F trio, and tapping a balanced range of human abilities not skewed disproportionately towards the cognitive domain.

If higher and further education are then assumed to have prime responsibility for full academic and vocational specialisation, a pictorial map of major educational aims by age and developmental stages can be drawn as overleaf, with examples of the appropriate topology of particular vocations being indicated.

Here full specialisation is depicted after a core experience of shared understandings and two transition periods as a range of 'teeth' leading out eventually to the research frontier in a particular area of experience, which in some fields at least might perhaps be depicted in award terms by the doctoral dissertation. The core of general education stresses a common culture which all men might share as brothers (which need not exclude as many subcultural variations which people individually or collectively might devise), rather than divisive cultures based upon social class or even race; the core is thus universal rather than elitist, but the picture recognises that differential competencies must be both recognised, respected and planned for certainly from the age of 15 or 16. The core exists not to promote a drab

Educational aims depicted pictorially by stages

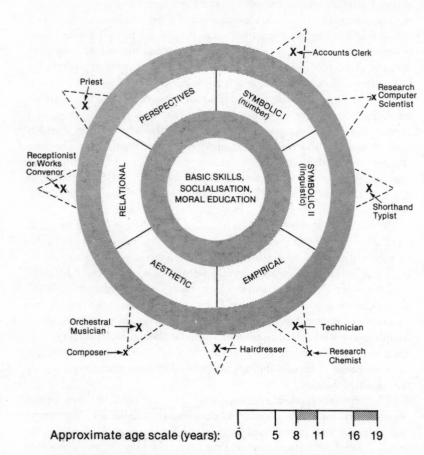

Approximate age scale (years):   0   5   8   11   16   19

(shaded boundaries are 'transition periods', and points of
dotted lines represent frontiers of human understanding)

		years
viz:	central core of basic skills (pre-school/infants)	0-8
	transition to cognitive differentiation (junior school)	8-11
	general, yet differentiated (secondary school)	11-16
	transition through limited specialisation	16-19
	specialised, tertiary academic/vocational	over 18 or 19 (approx)

The primary/secondary core is academic *and* social *and* practical.

uniformity and conformity, but to give all students more equal curricular opportunities to become different in terms of the total topology of their knowledge and skills and as a platform to which different specialists can return for successful cross-disciplinary communication.

The problem of general studies

In the traditional sixth form programme, the majority of students following the 3 A-level pattern have had around 30 per cent of the available timetabled periods for a combination of private study and often non-examined general-studies type courses, seminars, special guest lectures and the like. Superficially at least it appears that a great amount of time has been available within the existing arrangements for work which is not A-level related. The practical problem for teachers has, however, been to ensure that the one third non-examined time is used purposefully to attain its broadening objectives; frequently we know that this has failed to be the case, so that educators have felt it essential to continue general and liberal studies elements within further and higher education. (At Aston University, for example, all undergraduates, regardless of the faculty in which they are majoring, are in their first two years required to take for about three hours per week, an assessed programme of Complementary Studies. In the first year this consists of a well-planned series of major lectures by both outside speakers and university staff, followed by guided discussions in small groups. In their second year students select an optional specialist study from a wide range of courses available but which must not be directly related to the other main strands of their academic work.) As Maurice Holt makes clear in Chapter 6, only if general/liberal studies programmes 'can be made central to the students' whole curriculum can they generate the engagement upon which the process of education depends' . . . the objective is to extend the student's 'understanding of himself and his cultural inheritance by relating it intimately to his present concerns and future ambitions.'

Realistically, for both teachers and taught, it seems only common sense to recognise that if we espouse particular educational aims and set up procedures whereby their attainment is monitored, whether internally or externally as part of the total accounting system, we must either assess *all* aspects with an equivalent seriousness or discard those aims which in practice we relegate to the point at which, in the face of other pressures, effective motivation for many students evaporates. One reason why the A-level system has come under its many-pronged attack is that we have failed to use seriously enough the 30 per cent or so non-examined time for the intellectually able sixth former. Also, what we fail to appreciate is that the A-level class time is frequently not used to its maximum efficiency by appropriate teacher preparation and work demand on students in lessons and homework, so that two years of 7 or 8 periods per week remains for many students a slower pace than they could sustain. By appropriate selection from existing syllabuses (rather than total coverage) and professional demands on themselves and students a number of teachers still take some students from O to A-level in *one* year with good grades to show for their joint efforts.

The important point being made here is that the traditional sixth form curriculum pattern is not as intensive as is often assumed simply on the basis of its 3 subject specialisation; indeed to obtain say 6 or 7 O-level passes at one sitting may well be more difficult for many students than 3 at A-level. Hence there is time already available for adequate attention to necessary sixth form balancing components, whether or not new national qualification patterns emerge. The possible range of contents within general studies type courses is immense. Here, however, one rather unique course presently available within the International Baccalaureate will be briefly described since its main intention is to give a broad perspective on the totality of a general education curriculum having limited specialisation.

The Theory of Knowledge Course within the International Baccalaureate

The International Baccalaureate (IB) is a two-year programme for the age range under discussion which leads to higher education entry qualifications on a worldwide basis. It grew initially out of the needs of international schools which cater chiefly for children whose parents' work demands international mobility, but in terms of the analysis of a broad-based non-elitist general education discussed in this chapter its only major difference is its bilingual character which is reflected in the demands of the full Diploma examination (see below).

The IB is intended to give students a comparatively broad background, avoiding both an encyclopaedic approach and premature specialisation. A wide choice of options and levels within a firm general scheme of six subject areas makes the programme adaptable to the interests and needs of individual students. A basic course on the theory of knowledge, compulsory for all diploma candidates, aims to give coherence to the whole scheme. The common core in history and geography ensures an openminded approach and mutual understanding while studies in depth on a regional basis allow better acquaintance with local conditions. A summary structure of the general scheme for the IB Diploma is now given; satisfactory performance (measured on a 7 point scale) is required in six subject areas:

1. Mother tongue, including a syllabus of World Literature in translation.
2. A foreign language or second mother tongue.
3. Mathematics (varied syllabuses).
4. Experimental sciences; one of the following: biology, physics, chemistry, physical science, scientific studies.
5. Study of man; one of the following: history, geography, economics, philosophy, psychology, social anthropology.
6. One of the following: Art (art and design or music), a third language (classical or modern), a second subject from the study of man, a second subject from the experimental sciences, further mathematics, or an approved syllabus submitted by the school.

Three of these six subjects have to be offered at higher level, and three at subsidiary level, and *all* candidates must have followed a common course in the theory of knowledge and engaged satisfactorily in creative, aesthetic or social activities for about half a day per week. (Candidates may also offer single subjects for which they receive certificates rather than the full diploma.)

The parallels between this *grouped* examination structure and the previously outlined characteristics of general education are clear, and the opportunity to offer courses at either 'higher' or 'subsidiary' levels has parallels with the N/F proposals and ensures a justified limited specialisation for the age group. The scheme ensures that 'minority time' is taken seriously and there is thus less danger of undirected 'time filling'.

The *Theory of Knowledge* course (Whitfield 1976), which requires about 2 hours of class time per week for 2 years (or its equivalent) is intended to give *perspective* to the knowledge and understanding which students either already have or are acquiring in the rest of their studies. Its syllabus sections parallel in most respects the main curriculum structure, and are chiefly 'philosophical' in character, promoting students' abilities of 'second order' *reflection* and interrelation of what they might otherwise view as discrete and unconnected experiences in the bulk of their timetables. Furthermore it may be argued that to attain any degree of real mastery and understanding in any field, the philosophical character of the field should at least in outline be properly understood; one paradox of our existing curricular arrangements is that it is possible to gain even a first class honours degree in science or psychology for example without having any real literacy in the philosophy of science or of psychology.

The Theory of Knowledge course is thus not intended to teach students new facts, but to enable them to put into perspective and better understand what they already know. It may be taught on a team basis by people who do not have a university training in philosophy but share a common interest in:

(a) the basic concepts and conceptual structures of fields and forms of experience;
(b) the nature of the methods employed;
(c) the type of evidence appealed to as a basis for fact or opinion or belief;
(d) the degree of certainty with which conclusions may be stated; and
(e) the relationships between different disciplines and kinds of experience

(see also criteria (a) to (d) on page 61). In other words the teaching team need to share a concern for the conceptual and evidential basis upon which man makes sense of his condition through the various forms of thought and experience. Most schools appoint a course chairman or coordinator.

Internal, yet moderated student assessment has been based upon the criterion of students' *capacities to demonstrate deliberate, personal yet structured reflective analysis on knowledge and experience* using the following guidelines:

 (i) clarity or oral work in class presentations and discussion (20 per cent);
 (ii) understanding reading assignments (20 per cent);
(iii) written assignments: project folders, essays, textual criticism, test questions (50 per cent);
(iv) committment to the course, e.g. via extra voluntary work (10 per cent).

External examination papers have also been set with qualified success, bearing in mind the ambitiousness of the course objectives, and extra curriculum development for the course is still required to provide teachers and students with further necessary support materials; resources for such a task have not however been forthcoming. The ideas enshrined within the course may however be easily adapted in contexts quite independent of the IB as a whole.

Conclusion

Whatever the future structures of the 16–19 curriculum, they must build upon the preceding stages of the educational system. While utilising the resources of curriculum development, they must offer choice without fragmentation, and diversity with some structured coherence.

But our social and economic context is changing rapidly, and we have yet to characterise what curricular balance should mean in these circumstances. Can the educational system respond swiftly enough to the new demands being made upon it? Can it prepare youngsters with an adequate range of skills, couched within *flexible* attitudes towards their use, as marked structural unemployment of the under 25s stares us in the face within the immediate future? Can it act as a preventive force within the turmoil of family stress and instability which threatens daily the character and quality of the lives of a large proportion of our nation? Can the 16–19 phase prepare its students adequately for *interlinking* work at home (parenting etc), work in external employment, lifelong education and the responsible use of leisure?

I answer each of these questions 'possibly', but a precondition for that kind of response by the education service is a new and much more widely shared social and political dynamic based upon Christian and humanitarian ideals. In the rediscovery of such a dynamic, time may well not be on our side, yet as educators we have a crucial responsbility in prompting and helping our political masters to search for it.

5

The Sixth-Form Curriculum in Transition

These are uncertain times for the school sixth form. The harsher economic climate has made sixth forms of much less than a hundred pupils look vulnerable, and the effect of falling school rolls is still to come. Maintaining sixth-form staffing levels is not easy, and youth unemployment can have unpredictable effects on numbers. And if the present does not hold enough problems, there is the future of CEE, A-level and other examination proposals to debate and contemplate.

To some extent the next few years can be viewed together, for 16–19 numbers will continue to rise until 1983, and the schools must hope to be thus insulated from other influences which might reduce their sixth-form rolls to dangerously low levels. But the mid-1980s will bring ever fewer students, and the possibility of examination reform. Meanwhile, it is likely that economic pressures will have created more separate 16–19 institutions at the expense of school sixth forms, and the move towards a common 11–16 curriculum may have made a break at 16 look more acceptable as an educational proposition. There are signs, too, that the 16–19 sector will at least attract greater attention than in the last five years, and might at last be the subject of a commission of inquiry. Against this backdrop, schools must quicken their responses to the complex challenge of sixth form teaching and show that they can offer programmes that deserve a future in ten years' time.

We need first to decide what might be the attributes of a soundly-run sixth form; then we can see how far present practice measures up to this, and consider the likely effects of modifications to it. We can then suggest strategies which make the best use of the resources available to the school.

Characteristics of sixth-form education

It is a peculiarity of English schools that the sixth form is considered to offer a distinctive education in its own right. This influences our judgment of what other kinds of 16–19 institutions can provide, and it is arguable, too, that it has influenced 11–16 education. There are strong historical reasons for this, and we have already noted that the tradition of specialisation as the key to grammar-school sixth-form scholarship was borrowed from the Victorian public school. We have noted, too, that 'study in depth' has remained a continuing theme whenever the sixth form curriculum comes under review, and may therefore suggest that the first dimension of sixth-form quality is to do with curriculum design, and in particular with aspects of *specialisation* and the relation between breadth and depth of study. The key questions here are: is the curriculum broad enough to offer the student a reasonable cultural perspective, yet capable of demanding a rigorous understanding of a more limited area?

We have seen that in nineteenth-century Europe, the emphasis across the Channel was chiefly on cultural breadth; here it was on rigour and depth, and this resulted from the close and historically critical link between the Victorian public school and the universities of Oxford and Cambridge. English and Welsh (but not Scottish) secondary education took its pattern not, as in France and Germany, from the evolving elementary schools and the wide-ranging needs of mass education but from a school system designed to cater for an intellectual and social elite. Its two concerns have been summarised as godliness and good learning. The latter implied success at university entrance, and entailed close study of a narrow field; the former became a strong force from the mid-century onwards, as the ideals of Arnold's Rugby spread through the system, and piety went hand in hand with empire building. The order of Arnold's three aims shows a significant shift from the scholarship that had earlier been Butler's concern at Shrewsbury: 'First, religious and moral principles; secondly, gentlemanly conduct; thirdly, intellectual ability' (quoted in Percival 1969). By requiring sixth formers to be moral exemplars, Arnold gave them a new respectability, and an important role in fulfilling his aims for the whole school, while themselves benefiting from the noble station to which they had been called. This tradition, too, was assimilated by the 1904 grammar schools; religious links were often sought with the parish church, even if quite absent from the foundation statutes. And if the new schools could not afford the chaplains and chapels of the independent boarding schools, the prefects could at least read the lessons at morning assembly. Furthermore, they could help run the Muggleton County Grammar School, just as Tom Brown had eventually helped run Rugby. There were custodial duties in and around the school, promotion prospects in the cadet corps, and house teams to organise: the house system was a popular transplant, although without boarders there was little but competitive games to justify it. Even so, inter-house play competitions are a feature of life in many present-day comprehensive schools.

The name of this particular game was, and to some extent still is, leadership: although Arnold's concern was less with responsibility for others, more with 'Christian humility and personal integrity' (Percival). We could widen the concept and suggest that the second dimension of the sixth form is a desirable kind of *interaction*: a sense in which the sixth former benefits partly by social and intellectual contact with his contemporaries, but also by an engagement with the life and work of the main school. Key questions are: is there an opportunity for leadership? What is the influence of the sixth form on the tone of the school?

Finally, we note that good learning is not merely a matter of studying the right subjects for appropriate lengths of time. The process must have also an intensive quality, so that the young mind is not only nourished with facts, but also enabled to acquire skills of the intellect. Our third dimension will therefore be *quality of study*, and to assess this we must ask not what is being learnt, but how it is being learnt.

But this is, of course, a *post factum* analysis. No sixth form programme has ever been put together starting with these desirable elements. The sixth form curriculum is determined by its examination structure, and for conventional two-year students, the style of GCE A-level is the paramount influence on sixth-form life and work. The three A-level pattern makes it both easy and profitable to specialise, since the test applied to subject choice is not to look for balance or variety, but to ask: will this combination be negotiable currency when it comes to getting on a degree course?

General studies and specialisation

So the status and quality of general studies courses must come in for scrutiny if we are to look at ways in which the opportunities A-level offers for specialised study are compensated by minority-time activities. A survey in 1976 by the General Studies Association found that 'a planned course of general studies is not the norm', and although nearly 60 per cent of the schools surveyed claimed to have a common core course, most of these considered that physical and religious education, together with complementary courses like arts for scientists, were good enough. And courses said to be common to all students turned out often to be selective. This confirms the impression given by the Schools Council Sixth Form Survey (1970), which found that 47 per cent of sixth formers were spending less than 18 per cent of the week on non-examination work. More recently, Schools Council *Examinations Bulletin 38* (1978) found that 'over half the schools in the sample spent less than 10 per cent of their sixth-form teaching time on non-examined subjects', and this squares with the average figure of about 12 per cent found in the schools represented at the Cambridge sixth-form conferences (see Preface). But the figure of 30 per cent is still widely quoted, possibly echoing the one-third proportion of the 1961 Agreement to Broaden the Curriculum. The N and F proposals argue that the new examinations can be contained in 25 out of 35 weekly periods, leaving just over 28 per cent for 'work outside the study of main subjects'. But the Cambridge data suggest that most sixth-form staff would regard this as an unrealistically high figure if a five-subject curriculum is to be made to work.

In 1972, Fogelman studied a random sample of 1000 comments from the replies to a questionnaire sent to 15,000 students who had recently left school sixth forms. Almost all the comments were critical, and reading them is a useful corrective for complacency about the present state of the school sixth. As well as dissatisfaction with poor careers advice and petty restrictions, the narrowness of the curriculum came in for critical attention:

> I was not allowed to take biology, art and English as I wished. Hence I took biology, chemistry and physics and have regretted it ever since.

> There is too much specialisation, not enough projects outside the classroom, too much dependence on a narrow education system, not enough illumination of the main problems of existence.

Some schools have concluded that to make minority-time courses effective, the only answer is to examine them. A number of boards offer examinations at both A-level and AO-level, and in at least one 13–18 school, the AO-level is taken after one year in the sixth, and the A-level for most students in the second year. A report in *Dialogue* (Spring 1977) outlines some topic-centred approaches to A-level general studies courses. In the London Board's proposals, each student would choose two large topics from: one earth, France, perception, science and society, development studies, the Great War and European civilisation. The new departure here is the provision by the board itself of teaching materials. And in a proposal (as yet unimplemented) by the Joint Matriculation Board for an alternative general-studies A-level, six topics are specified: the romantic revolution (focus, William Blake); science, ethics and society; energy- resources and usage; third-world development (focus, Sri Lanka); mass media (focus, censorship); living in towns. It is worth noting, too, that the Schools Council has commissioned two N/F-level 'feasibility studies': in one of these, for example, an N-level in general studies would be obtained by selecting three topics out of these eight: cities, conflicts and society, the arts and social change, computers and society, communications, population, energy resources and their usage, and the age of romanticism and revolution. Balance, in this scheme, is imposed by giving each topic a number score under each of the headings: arts, social science, natural science. The student must then choose his three topics so as to ensure a score within given limits under each heading. The demise of N and F may well promote a revival of interest in 'balanced' general studies schemes.

Examined general studies are certainly likely to be taken seriously by staff, and the Schools Council General Studies Project concluded, in *Working Paper 25* (1969), that 'if the staff recognise that general studies are important and part of the normal programme, so will the students'. This project was, however, concerned with them as a non-examined component, and suggested that general studies should display three distinct characteristics. First, the topics should have such general significance as to require study by all students: second, whatever is being studied should 'establish general connexions' so that interesting byways may be explored: and third, there should be 'general transfer' between what is learnt and a wider area of experience. The published materials are thematically organised, and can be used by schools at their own discretion rather than in a rigidly recommended style (as, for example, with the Humanities Curriculum Project materials).

In addition to these initiatives, the General Studies Association has for some years published a regular journal devoted to the furtherance of the concept and based on school experience. Even so, the Cambridge conferences showed that while teachers considered one-year courses the most pressing sixth-form problem, the next for the sample surveyed was to establish a sound general studies programme. The participants showed much variation in practice, with as few as one or as many as 12 periods being given to general studies, with coherent course planning in a minority of schools, and optioned, topic-based courses much in evidence. Only 19 per cent considered that the provision for general studies in their schools was satisfactory.

The two standard excuses for this state of affairs would refer to the lack of resources for staffing general studies well, and the unsympathetic attitude of students. But resources are a matter of curriculum priorities; and the Sixth Form Survey of the Schools Council found that 43 per cent of sixth formers would like to spend more time on general studies. It is difficult to avoid the conclusion that while heads of schools will profess support for general studies, they are not prepared to make them important enough to matter. It is too easy to bundle together the offcuts from the timetable, and persuade a few staff with free periods and an interesting hobby that they can run a half-term course based on it, or on 'current affairs', or some other generalised topic that can be boned up from a couple of books, and padded out with a film and perhaps a visiting speaker. Simply add a games afternoon shared with the fifth year, and allow any interested students to paint or throw pots for a couple of periods, and the result will look good in the prospectus. The underlying assumption is, stated baldly, that the sixth form can more or less look after itself, and it is worth noting that only a third of the Cambridge conference teachers had a responsibility in the sixth form that was exclusive of other duties.

A good general studies programme may, in fact, take no more staffing to mount; but it needs much more planning and preparation, and is unlikely to happen unless an able teacher is given the paid responsibility for it, along with some money for resources and space of some kind for storing them. Then a team of committed staff can be set up, and written into the timetable at an early stage so that general studies periods are inviolable. It is not good enough for heads and tutors to say that these periods are important: sixth formers will need to see that they are important. The work of the projects already quoted suggests that the lineaments of an effective scheme are pretty obvious, without the need for very much speculation. After all, the 'general significance' of *Working Paper 25* rested both on the teacher's judgment and on what 'any reasonable person would consider significant'.

It is convenient to think in terms of an optional and a mandatory component. The former would include games activities, unless the choice offered was wide enough to suggest that it was not unreasonable to expect every student to do something. In the light of evidence showing the adult connexion between health and fitness, thought should be given to the case for offering all students a basic keep-fit course. Physical education departments can too readily assume that all a sixth former needs is a choice between team games and activities like golf or sailing. A well-organised short session of the kind of exercises that students should find time for when they take up full-time employment might prove a popular element in an afternoon of recreational activities. A further one or two periods could be given to options on the practical side of the creative and expressive areas. As well as the arts and crafts activities, there is scope for music and drama: in general, for the performance subjects.

The mandatory part of general studies would have a team-based, thematic approach and select topics likely to appeal to the staff involved, and to have an open-enough texture to allow the easy pursuit of related matters in response to the interests of students. In practice, as we have seen, these topics will be drawn from the arts, sciences and social studies areas, but the planning team will ensure that they can incorporate those kinds of understanding which, taken together, represent the broad sweep of our culture. For instance, the 'central studies' planning team at one school (Holt 1978) began work after all the staff, at a residential week-end conference, had given their support to a sixth-form programme which made this a compulsory element for all students, along with a more flexible approach to the timetabling of examination work. Topics such as aspects of a technological society, crime, democracy east and west, were mapped on to the curriculum areas already established in the common 11–16 curriculum—

the areas of expressive arts, maths and science, design, and humanities and social studies. Thus the theme of 'conflict' might be exploited as the study of the novel or poem with a war background; genetics and chemical warfare; conflict in art appreciation; race relations; and a sociological study of the family. Democracy would involve censorship and the media; power in society; the role of the artist; responsibilities of the scientist; the planned economy and free enterprise. A team of staff was assembled with an overall staffing ratio of one to ten or twelve students, and including representative and enthusiastic staff from all faculties. Room was found in the library stock room for filing cabinets and trays, and money made available for the purchase of relevant units from the Schools Council General Studies Project, as well as the development of school-based resources using the school offset litho machine. A senior member of staff was given charge of the programme, and coordinated the arrangements for outside speakers, visits, films and so on.

In a week of twenty 70-minute periods, one single and one double were blocked out for central studies at an early stage in the construction of the blocked timetable. To this 15 per cent of the time were added optional periods for recreational activities, for creative arts, and for expressive arts: and a further compulsory period was given over to advice on careers, and on living in society (mortgages, hire purchase, social services, consumer issues). Thus a minimum of 20 per cent of minority-time study could rise to 35 per cent, and every care was taken to ensure that the compulsory minimum offered a pattern of built-in choice so as to give the best chance of involving all students. Experience suggests that a scheme of this kind can sustain a much higher engagement with students than those which depend on an extrinsic choice between mini-courses, put together on the basis of staff availability and interest rather than a coherent scheme for worthwhile study. This particular scheme was not examined: but a choice exists of schemes on similar lines which lead to public examinations at AO or A-level. It is unwise to be doctrinaire on the merits of an examination link. It is unquestionably possible to devise a sound and popular course without recourse to it, and one thus gains an extra degree of freedom. But the ethos of a particular school may mean that staff energies can only be mobilised if the examination incentive is offered. The common prerequisite is staff involvement in the enterprise, and this will be needed whether the course is examined or not.

Interactions with school and community

Another element of a general studies programme could be some form of social or public service within the school's community, and this brings us to the second dimension of the traditional sixth form: of interaction within the student body and outside it. We have seen that this arose from religious and moral considerations in the Victorian public school. It is likely that its adoption by the maintained grammar schools led, through the notion of the house system, to the growth of pastoral care in the 11–16 school as comprehensive education was extended during the 1960s. But, as Lacey's study (1970) makes clear, the grammar school used the house system as an organisational rather than a social device. At Hightown Grammar, the houses

> formed the basis for registration, for the distribution of free milk at morning break, and for dinners at mid-day. In addition, one morning assembly a week was given over to house prayers, conducted by the housemaster, and various games, scholastic competitions (debates, declamations) and charity activities were organised on a house basis. Finally, rewards and punishments (house points and detentions) were organised on a house basis too.

The academic organisation, after the first year, was kept quite separate, and the use of the house system to mediate the authority structure was unsoftened by the firm-but-gentle family feeling of the public school boarding house and its living-in housemaster. Furthermore, Lacey's book suggests a coldness about relations between staff and pupils: 'A number of ritualistic elements in the organisation of the school supported the persona and increased the role distance between teacher and pupil'. And although the growth of pastoral care in comprehensive schools has gone much further in respect of support structures and careers advice than anything in most grammar schools, it can amount to a development of system and mechanism rather than of the warmth of staff-student relationships. It is worth noting that the longitudinal study by Rutter *et al* (1979) revealed a negative relationship 'between pupil behaviour and the head teacher's pastoral emphasis as reported at interview'.

A related issue is the use of sixth formers as prefects. This can be justified by pointing to the supposed advantages of the interaction for both parties—the main-school pupils, and the sixth formers. The Rutter study, however, seems to suggest that it is advantageous to give responsibility and participation opportunities to a high proportion of the main-school pupils themselves:

> Schools in which a high proportion of children held some kind of position of responsibility in the school system had better outcomes with respect to both pupil behaviour and examination success.

Prefect systems tend to syphon off opportunities for pupils to chair committees, organise dances and charity events, serve on school councils and so on. But they remain popular: R King (1976) quotes a 1973 survey of 72 schools, of which only 4 claimed not to have prefects. At the 1977 and 1978 Cambridge conferences (see preface), prefects with 'custodial duties of some kind' were a feature of nearly half the schools represented. It is worth asking, though, how far such duties are a proper experience for a sixth former. However trivial the custodial duty, the prefect stands in place of the teacher and must exercise authority without benefit of the teacher's maturity, experience and commitment. Devising authority and participation structures for schools is no longer as straightforward as it was in Dr Arnold's day, and a further disadvantage is that the school with prefects must also have non-prefects. If there are pupils whose business is to enforce rules, others will make it their business to break them.

There is much to be said for encouraging those sixth formers so inclined to interact with the main school by taking part in clubs, games, societies, and form and year activities. They might help run the second-year dance or the third-year play; help with remedial reading (under appropriate direction) or with year assemblies. There is scope, too, for greater involvement with the main school curriculum: for example, a sixth former reading A-level history might have a couple of free periods that coincide with the fourth year humanities programme, and could act as an ancillary to the staff team with genuine mutual benefit. But the truth is that the greater maturity of our adolescents, and the decline of the inter-war hierarchical society in which the maintained grammar school developed and refined its prefect systems and uniform regulations, are inimical to extensive links between the sixth form and the main school. As Peterson wrote in 1973:

> Even if the selective 11–18 grammar school were not on its way out all over Europe, the long age range would be proving, as it is in those grammar schools which remain, unmanageable in conditions where staying on into the sixth form is the rule rather than the exception. Thus we see in more and more of our remaining grammar schools, as in comprehensives, the creation of a 'sixth form block' and the treatment of the sixth form as a separate entity within the school, rather than an integrated 'top' to a unified society.

We are left with interactions between the students themselves, and with the community outside the school. In these respects school sixth forms stand on all fours with separate 16–19 institutions, and these aspects are discussed in the next chapter. But it is worth observing that in the sixth form itself, the quality of staff-student relations will determine the quality of inter-student relations, and the school ought to be able to engender an affectionate tolerance of eccentricity, a scholar's taste for informed discussion, more readily perhaps than in a student body of ten times the size, and including the whole range of abilities and interests. But this is to imply a more open relationship between staff and students than one observes in some schools. And as for community links, it is not enough to concoct a list of old ladies' overgrown gardens and undecorated parlours; the evidence is that these personal contacts should be regular if they are to do much good, and organising them properly is demanding to the students and time-consuming for staff. Community action projects also need detailed planning, and if a choice has to be made, it might be wiser to revivify general studies than divert effort to what is desirable but possibly peripheral.

Curriculum, organisation and quality of study

The third suggested dimension is that of quality of study, and in tertiary education the critical balance must be struck between formal content—in which A-level syllabuses usually abound—and informal discussion and argument. Wankowski (1974) classified A-level tuition as two-way or one-way, depending on whether it did, or did not, provide a 'positively encouraging atmosphere for discussion and questioning'. Even in science subjects, students taught by two-way methods gained higher A-level grades, and were associated with 'a higher standard of achievement at degree level'. Fogelman's study (1972) showed that sixth formers had difficulty adapting to independent work after the spoon-feeding of their O-level courses in the main school. This shows that continuity of school study—a particular aim of the GCE system on its introduction—has suffered from the increasing emphasis on examination at 16-plus. It suggests, too, that one of the chief arguments used to justify 11–18 education in the same institution may have little substance in it. We could turn the continuity argument on its head, and say that since schools have allowed a discontinuity to develop at 16-plus, the stimulus of a move to another institution might help students overcome it.

It seems a pity that so few schools have adopted a fourth and fifth year curriculum which allows the assessment of course work to count towards GCE and CSE grades. Then the pattern of independent study can be established and rewarded in preparation for post-16 education. Generally, though, this requires a Mode 3 approach, with more work for both teachers and—contrary to popular belief—pupils too. Another factor is increasing competition for good A-level grades, which tends to affect arts students most keenly. It becomes risky to explore the unexpected idea, the unread author. On the other hand, Nuffield A-level science courses, which generally stress the Popperian approach of conjecture and refutation, depend upon critical inquiry for their success. It is possible that in at least some schools, the science teaching is imaginative and unfettered, and the arts students the prisoners of set notes and received opinion—the reverse of what one might expect.

This issue is linked with the way available teaching resources are used. A major question is the number of different A-level subjects to offer, and there seems little point in schools overstretching themselves in vain attempts to compete with the 25 to 30 subjects that most 16–19 colleges can muster. The first rule of survival is to fight battles one can win: this is one schools can only lose. It is better to offer a smaller choice but teach them really well. The DES recommendation is for a minimum of 16 subjects at A-level, and a sixth form of 120 should be able to manage this given the usual sixth form staffing ratio of one teacher to 10 or 12 students. Smaller sixth forms might aim for 12; after all, the leading ten subjects provide 80 per cent of all A-level entries. These are, for summer 1977 (the latest available DES statistics), with the most popular first: mathematics (all kinds); English; physics; economics (including economic history); biology (including botany and zoology); history; chemistry; geography; general studies; and art. The chief surprise here is the disappearance of French from the top ten, hitherto in ninth place. In yielding to general studies, it confirms both the failing appeal of modern languages and the growing tendency to make general studies an examined subject. Other subjects which have lost ground over the three years 1975–7 are history and geography, while economics and biology have moved up. That biology should displace chemistry as the second science subject is particularly interesting. Overall, the growing support for science subjects seems to be confirmed. The continuing pre-eminence of mathematics over English may seem remarkable, but it squares with one of the results of Reid's interesting study (1972)—that in terms of the acceptability of A-level subjects by university admissions tutors, mathematics tops the list of subjects in which, regardless of university course, 'a pass at A-level would definitely be acceptable if offered by an applicant for admission'. It is instructive to rearrange the ten most popular specialist subjects in order of acceptability. The result is: mathematics, physics, chemistry, history, biology, geography, French, English, economics and art. The first few scores are quite close, but English has only two-thirds the acceptability of mathematics, and art little more than a third. The low acceptability of economics has not inhibited its rise from seventh place in 1975 to fourth place in 1977.

So far the choice of A-level subjects is straightforward. Trouble starts in selecting the minority subjects. Some, like British Constitution, have an over-lap with one of the 'big ten' and count as luxuries in the small school. The difficulty is that German, religious knowledge, home economics and music are perfectly distinct and, furthermore, are likely to be taught to O-level. One solution is to offer them between a group of schools or institutions, and I shall consider this approach shortly. If the solution is to be found within the school, three devices are commonly employed. The first is to join together the lower and upper-sixth sets in a subject for all or part of the time, and for the schools represented at the Cambridge conferences, 4 schools out of 5 in the sample did this for minority time A-levels. The second is to run these subjects with a reduced period allocation, and this happened in half the schools. Finally, one can run them with some of the teaching done after or before school, or at lunch time: only one in three schools resorted to this. A majority of the school representatives considered that the provision for minority A-levels was not satisfactory; but only a third of the schools made use of all three devices (including the option of cooperation with other schools).

It looks as if there is scope for development here, and it is worth bearing in mind that both the quantity and quality of A-level teaching are important. Christie and Oliver (1969) analysed A-level grades in relation to teaching time allocation, and showed that beyond about four hours a week in a given subject, more time does not lead to better grades. Beyond a certain point, 'time on task' seems not to have the effect noticed by researchers into the performance of younger children. A key factor, as Richard Whitfield points out in Chapter 4, is to sustain the intensity of learning. Hence the importance of student motivation, and it is interesting to note that Vincent and Dean (1977) found that one-year A-level students 'appeared to be more vocationally oriented'. Most of these were found to be in colleges of further education which were running these intensive courses with a substantial degree of success.

Time saved on examination work is a useful bonus for general studies. The Cambridge data suggest a working week of 1400 minutes is the rule in most schools, although the range of allocations from 1225 to 1600 minutes is striking. There is evidently a good deal of latitude here, and cropping only 20 minutes off total weekly class-contact time in a school with 60 staff makes available another 34 periods of 35 minutes, every week: valuable for extra teaching or, in particular, curriculum planning. In most schools there are 40 periods of 35 minutes weekly, and usually 8 periods are allocated to each A-level subject. This gives a total of 280 minutes: 40 minutes more than research suggests is necessary. It looks as if the normal allocation should be 7 and not 8 periods. It looks, too, as if even more over-teaching is the general rule, for Table II.14 of *Examinations Bulletin 38* (which looked at 189 schools) shows that the average proportion of the week spent on teaching three A-levels is 67.6 per cent, which in a 1400 minute week gives 315 minutes per subject.

It would be wrong to suggest that 240 minutes per week is a magic figure for all or, indeed, for any subjects; some might need more, and others might manage on less. But neither is 315 minutes a magic figure; and it is not unreasonable to conclude that much could be done to make A-level teaching more cost effective. If schools expect to retain sixth forms, they must also expect a closer study of how their resources are deployed. In large sixth forms, for example, students can be given a wide choice of A-level subject combinations by grouping them into 3 or even 4 columns; indeed, this is to some extent a timetabling convenience. But in the smaller school it becomes a timetabling penalty, particularly if a common curriculum from 11 to 16 requires a blocked structure in years 1 to 5. A better solution is to establish which subject combinations are desired by the incoming lower sixth (after discussion with parents, career staff and tutors), and write in the A-level subject periods which make these combinations possible. Moreover, additional flexibility can be gained (and this may be useful if a common-core general studies scheme is planned) if the timetabling of A-level periods recognises the value of a tutorial approach in sixth form work. Thus six 35-minute periods might be timetabled as written-in fixed contact time, and the seventh period (which would be an accepted part of the teacher's load) could be arranged between teacher and students in a variety of ways. It could be fitted in as a personal supervision period for each student, or possibly a pair of students, in a lunch hour or before school; and it would serve to introduce the student to university styles of teaching. The principle could perhaps be extended further in teaching groups with small numbers of students, along with a reduction in total time allocation. In the popular subjects, Examinations Bulletin 38 shows that even a sixth form in the 10–50 size band might have 18 takers for A-level English literature, and suggests that 'The point at which groups are split seems somewhere between 12 and 14'. The schools in the Cambridge sample, however, had maximum groups with a mean size of 20, and almost all schools had groups bigger than 16: the mean sixth form size was 130. There seems no reason why groups should not rise to 20 or so, if this makes it possible to use staffing effectively in other ways in the sixth form. If the burden of, say, reading English essays is severe, it will be cheaper to allow the teacher an extra free period than originate a second set. But if staffing permits, a second set allows a wider combination of A-level subjects.

Provision for one-year students

We turn now from a consideration of two-year students to look at the curriculum provision for other sixth formers. Schools Council Examinations Bulletin 38 estimates that about two-thirds of the sixth form will be taking A-levels over two years, with about 27 per cent taking just three A-levels; as many again combining these with O-levels, CSE or CEE; and about 14 per cent taking only two A-levels along with these exams. Only 5 per cent will take just 1 A-level + O/CSE/CEE, so there will be altogether about half the lower sixth taking O-level, CSE or CEE along with at least one A-level. This leaves about a quarter made up of one-year students only, and Vincent and Dean's figure of 27 per cent (Chapter 3) tallies with this. Really, though, we have a continuum of students, and division by exam category reflects the extent to which exams dominate the sixth-form curriculum. Although A-level in at least one subject is part of the programme for three-quarters of the average lower-sixth form, its failure rate shows that more is being expected of this examination, and the kind of course it gives rise to, than it can effectively deliver.

The ineffectiveness of O-level for one-year students—documented by Vincent and Dean (1977), and discussed in Chapter 3— is often masked by the greater success abler students have with it. These will generally be on two-year courses, but will take O-levels—often for the second time—after one year. Thus, for example, Rutter *et al* (1979) compared O-level performance for the whole of the lower sixth with that a year earlier, at the end of the fifth year, for twelve inner-London secondary schools. They found 'very substantial improvements in their final exam scores', the ablest increasing from 5.64 to 7.68 O-levels. The average O-level score on entry to the sixth was 3.00, and this had risen to 4.69 at the end of the first year. But if we look at one-year students only, as Vincent and Dean did, the corresponding figures found were 1.1 and 2.2. This is not really surprising; O-level is designed for the upper 20 per cent of the ability range. But it brings out the need for other kinds of one-year courses. One other result of the Rutter study should be mentioned: the performance of the lower sixth pupils showed marked differences depending on the school they attended, both at the end of the fifth year and after a year in the sixth. This is good news for students in good schools. But it also confirms the uplifting effect a break at 16 can have, if it allows the student to make a fresh start and escape from the effects of poor teaching or an uncongenial school climate. Another point is that the greater resources of separate 16–19 institutions allow them to offer a far wider range of O-levels, and so ring the changes on what students have already attempted. Even so, schools can take steps in this direction for the more popular subjects, and Vincent and Dean suggested that if more schools did so, the O-level success rate for one-year sixth formers might rise. Rather than repeat O-level mathematics, there is a case for trying accounts, economics or statistics.

Where does all this leave the schools? Even where suitable courses are to hand, few school sixth forms can command the resources to provide them in full measure. With an average sixth-form size of 81, and an average teaching group of 8 (*Education*, 1.6.79), there is little room for manoeuvre. As a first principle, then, schools must recognise that they may not be able to offer a worthwhile course—one which significantly enhances his understanding of our culture, and better equips him to make his way in the world—to every pupil who seeks entry to the sixth form at the end of the fifth year. The school's resources must therefore be allocated to courses in an order of priority, and most schools and parents would agree that some basic provision for A-level courses will be essential. But how far this is extended to the less popular subjects will depend on the range of students, and the other facilities available in the area. It must be recognised, too, that for many students at present taking two-year A-level courses, the failure rate suggests that A-level is not a suitable course. And unless some kind of intermediate or lower-level course, like a suitably designed N-level, is accessible, then at least some of these students might be better advised to take an OND or BEC/TEC Diploma course at a tertiary or further education college.

If we turn to one-year courses, we need to stress this second principle: in deciding what to offer, the school must have regard to its own resources, the other facilities of the area, and its responsibilities to its pupils which cannot be adequately met elsewhere. We can again agree that some basic provision for O-level courses will be essential. But beyond this, the decision to embark on CEE or foundation courses will take account of what other schools and colleges are doing. For example, a developing comprehensive school in an outer London borough, planning its future sixth form provision, noticed that other schools were relying heavily on O-level for one-year courses, with mediocre results. But there were likely to be a large proportion of one-year students, and the nearest FE college was some distance away. The area had a high unemployment rate, but inquiries initiated by the school staff with local firms showed considerable interest in City and Guilds foundation courses. A major programme to mount these courses and develop appropriate curriculum materials was therefore carried through, and the proportion of fifth-year pupils staying on is over twice the average figure of 20 per cent for the other schools in the neighbourhood.

On the other hand, a former rural grammar school turned comprehensive had a strong demand for one-year courses in conventional subjects, and added a range of CEE subjects—art, home economics, technical studies, geography, English, social studies—to its O-level subjects, along with RSA typing and shorthand and other business studies subjects, and CSEs in accounts and additional maths. Careful analysis over three years showed that a generous allocation of time to each subject—4 or 6 periods of 50 minutes each—improved exam performance; and also that it was better to structure the subjects around a vocational theme, rather than offer them in random columns. Thus there is one general course, one for pre-nursing, a secretarial course, and a business studies course. Another school, however, found its limited resources were overstretched by an extensive CEE programme, at the expense of general studies. It reduced the number of CEE subjects and extended further its links with the FE college only two miles away.

For comprehensive schools, thinking along these lines can mean hard decisions; the tradition of open access is a worthy one. But unless the resources are there to sustain it and give students a decent course, the policy may be doing some of them a disservice. What is proposed here is not, however, an ability bar; it is possible that a school might decide that while the local FE college can offer adequate courses for the middle range of one-year students, its weakness lies in providing for those with only a few lowish CSE passes, and who may be temperamentally unsuited to life in a large institution. The school might then concentrate on the extremes: a good range of A and O-level courses, and one or two carefully designed foundation courses, or perhaps a range of Mode 3 CEE subjects, for its post-16 students in need of a particularly supportive structure. It is worth adding that some sixth-form colleges have done pioneering work with students of this kind, for whom the conventional further education college has often provided very little. It should be remarked, too, that one in three of the schools represented at the Cambridge conferences had excluded some potential sixth-form students, and most required 3 or 4 O-levels from aspiring three A-level candidates.

In all this, we assume that the school not only knows its pupils, but also knows about the opportunities open to them and, by means of its careers and guidance service, makes the necessary connections. But a survey of 250 teenagers who left school in summer 1977, commissioned from Youthaid by the Employment Directorate of the EEC, showed 'a lack of knowledge "across the board" about the type of job opportunities available . . . The aims of schools were so varied they were almost contradictory' (*Education*, 5.1.79). And as the number and type of post-16 courses increase, so the picture becomes more confusing for leavers and students. There is scope for great waste and muddle at the 16-plus transition point, and it can only be reduced by improving guidance from the third year onwards. Again, it is evident that post-16 performance is a function largely of 11–16 school experience.

Cooperative schemes for schools and colleges

Whatever new examinations lie in the future, the indisputable fact which faces many schools with sixth forms is that after numbers reach their peak in 1982–3, they will begin to fall. And even before then, pressures to rationalise 16–19 education and simplify the array of competing courses and institutions will threaten many sixth forms. There are two ways in which matters might be resolved. One is to separate the sixth forms from the schools and form a separate 16–19 college, and this is examined in the next chapter. The other is to persuade school sixth forms either to work together, so that both minority A-levels and one-year courses can be efficiently planned and staffed; or to work in conjunction with other kinds of 16–19 institution. A third possibility would apply only in remote rural areas, where the LEA would accept the lack of any alternative and give the school the extra staffing it needs to make a comprehensive sixth form work as well as possible.

Informal cooperation between schools is not easy to establish: it was practised by fewer than 1 in 3 of the schools represented at the Cambridge conferences. The mutual incompatibility of timetables is one stumbling block, but there is also the problem of the head of German or music who sees A-level work as the cream in his coffee. And in areas where secondary transfer works by parental choice, or where falling rolls have exacerbated inter-school competition, parents might assume that the school not offering A-level German is not as desirable as the one down the road that does.

The sixth-form centre is one way of avoiding some of these problems. That run by the Inner London Education Authority in Tower Hamlets works on the voluntary basis that if a contributing school cannot raise a group of more than five in a subject, then the students can travel to the centre to take it. The 17 schools in the division thus all retain their sixth forms, and the centre is run by a 'coordinator of studies': in this case, a senior teacher on a four-year secondment from one of the schools. Describing the scheme in the *Times Educational Supplement* (4.11.77), Patricia Rowan comments:

> It would certainly have been cheaper to turn one of the 17 small secondary schools of division five into a sixth-form centre or college if tangled competitive, political and union interests could have been unravelled. But the ILEA has shown in its 16–19 policy that it has no stomach for such a fight.

The Tower Hamlets scheme is also discussed by Lightfoot (1978), a former education officer of the ILEA. He regards such centres as 'more hopeful' than inter-school collaboration, but adds that 'in terms of utilisation of capital plant—buildings, laboratories, and so forth—it is comparatively expensive. In practical terms, the capital plant used for this purpose needs to be a net addition to that available at present . . .' The extra cost of sixth-form centres along the Tower Hamlets lines means that they are a fragile political compromise. Even without the distorting effects of parental choice, to make one school the 'mushroom' centre seems a poor educational idea, since the students do not all start off on equal social terms. The logic of a sixth-form or tertiary college solution is irresistible, and must be inevitable in the longer term. And it is worth noting that Vincent and Dean's work on one-year sixth formers (1977) found no evidence that these students were deterred from continuing their education by having to move to another institution.

A tempting possibility is closer cooperation between schools and FE colleges, and it is surprising how little many LEAs have done to bring it about. The future will see many more schemes of this kind. Oxfordshire has been a pioneering authority here, and R Wilcock, the former principal of the West Oxfordshire Technical College, has written (*The Times Educational Supplement*, 4.11.77) about the link between the college and four local 11–18 comprehensive schools which, from 1973, formed the West Oxfordshire Consortium. Considerable difficulties have emerged, chiefly because 'In effect, there has never been one body acting as such to carry out the stated objectives'. Even though the timetables of the five institutions were interlocked for part of the week, 'pupils in schools striving for sixth forms were found to adapt their A-level objectives to match the range of subjects available in their own school'.

Unless the LEA makes it plain that all the schools in the partnership are on equal terms, school autonomy—often with parental and staff support—will ultimately torpedo the hopes that inspire such schemes. With care, though, a federal scheme can work very well, and Appendix A gives details of the Cambridge Collegiate Board which was also formed in 1973, but which is 'enjoined by the Education Committee to monitor, guide and develop 16-plus education as a whole'. The board operates through two further education colleges, two sixth-form colleges, and two sixth forms in 11–18 schools—all in and around Cambridge—and consists of the principals of these six centres. Perhaps the key to the success of this scheme is that the board's secretary is full-time, and has headmaster status. Centre heads of department constitute subject panels for inter-centre liaison, and an overall contact ratio for all the centres is agreed with the local authority. For the area served by the board, 45 per cent of fifth-year students continue in full-time education, compared with a national figure of around 30 per cent. The board's secretary, Peter Bryan, has suggested six pre-requisites if federal schemes of this kind are to work. First, both school and FE institutions should be involved; second, each unit in the scheme should have a minimum of 200 students; third, each unit needs a guaranteed role; fourth, the implementing board must have binding powers; fifth, potential students must have full, free information about all courses; and finally, someone external to the contributing units should have the task of coordinating the whole.

In the transitional years ahead, the school sixth-form curriculum must inevitably be seen as simply one part of a unified 16–19 provision for a given area. There seems no good reason why the reform of A-level should be seen as a separate issue: it is arguable that this examination has had a mesmeric effect on schools, blinding them to the fact that even with this most academic of 16–19 programmes, competition from FE colleges has become stiffer over the years. And although the shortcomings of A-level choice and general studies schemes have been clearly chronicled in the Schools Council's 1970 Sixth Form Survey and in subsequent documents, schools have done little to improve their sixth-form arrangements.

A good example of compartmentalised thinking is the Schools Council's original proposal for one-year CEE courses, and two-year N-level courses, but with no link at all between them. Why suppose that one-year students will not turn into two-year students? If schools could learn from further education and develop one-year courses with not only their own surrender value, but also recognised value as the first stage of a two-year course, then a more flexible system would result and many students might be encouraged to stay on for a second sixth-form year. There is a reluctance, too, to accept that a course with a vocational theme can be organised so as to attract students, but offer enough generalised content to prevent an unduly narrow job orientation. It is easy to forget that traditional nineteenth-century classical education was certainly vocational—but the jobs it prepared sixth formers for have gone, and were, indeed, already going by the 1880s. A few men of vision, such as T H Huxley, recognised this and urged that science, for example, should become a part of both general education and liberal culture. But the issues were muddled, as Williams (1961) points out:

> The classical linguistic disciplines were primarily vocational, but these particular vocations had acquired a separate traditional dignity, which was refused to vocations now of equal human relevance. Thus, instead of the new learning broadening a general curriculum, it was neglected, and in the end reluctantly admitted on the grounds that it was of a purely technical kind.

The effect of the three A-level straitjacket is just as exclusive: mathematics and science are for specialists. They have no recognised place in the formal curriculum of students choosing arts subjects, and their wider historical and philosophical aspects are neglected even for science specialists. But further education experience shows that vocational alignment and curriculum breadth need not be mutually exclusive. Future attempts to re-think the sixth-form curriculum can no longer take place, like those incessant Schools Council working parties, in a private-party atmosphere. They must have regard not only to the pattern of FE courses and the vitality of tertiary colleges, but also to the new forms of education and training which are emerging from the initiatives of the Manpower Services Commission. But even without new curriculum approaches, there is a great deal schools can do to breathe life into sixth-form practice and procedures.

6
Tertiary and Sixth-Form Colleges

The growth of A-level courses in colleges of further education through the 1960s was a reflection both of changes in teenage culture and of the schools' sluggish response to these changes. As Owen (1977) has remarked, in considering the early days of the Schools Council, 'Few criticisms of schooling were expressed in the mid-sixties and even fewer were admitted to be true'. But students themselves had discovered an eloquent form of non-verbal criticism; in the swinging years of Beatlemania, uniforms and prefects took the shine off the virtues of staying put, except for the more academic types who, in the main, recognised shrewdly enough that schools had close links with universities, and that they could well profit from them.

For most school sixth forms, therefore, it was a matter of business as usual; it was easy enough to tolerate the odd non-conforming high-flier, when the very existence of dress regulations was enough to see off the long-haired divergers to the college down the road, and save the school from more trouble than they were worth. Numbers were increasing anyway, and with mounting competition for university places, schools might as well concentrate on what they could do well. And the results of the 1978 survey mentioned in the Preface show that change has been slow; well over a third of the schools represented at the Cambridge conferences retained sixth-form prefect systems and uniform regulations, and our present nostalgia for whatever politicians mean by 'standards' suggests that the proportion might even rise before it falls.

But in one important respect the clock cannot be turned back. In building up their full-time A-level students, the colleges not only gained more, initially, in prestige than the schools lost in Burnham unit totals; they also showed that the ambience of the school was not an essential accompaniment to the successful completion of academic courses. When Wearing King (1968) proposed the merger of Croydon's grammar-school sixth forms into a single 16–19 college in 1956, the councillors could accept the economic logic, but not the educational implications. Ten years later, comprehensive reorganisation faced Luton with the prospect of small school sixth forms, and the solution of a sixth-form college was perfectly palatable. Its local acceptance was eased by an insistence on four O-levels for admission, and an 'academic bias to the work of the college' (quoted in Macfarlane 1978). But the Department of Education and Science favoured a less restrictive entry policy, and open access was adopted for the three sixth-form colleges opened in Southampton in 1967. By 1969 ten were established, and by 1971 Luton had dropped its entry requirements. The tide had turned.

The original intention of Exeter's education committee in 1970 was to base a sixth-form college on the boys' grammar school (Merfield 1973). But a new building was in the course of construction at the city's technical college, and the committee noticed that the college had as many A-level students as the grammar school. A solution which would have been unthinkable in Luton a few years before, now appeared as the obvious way to avoid duplication of courses; the college could take over the function of the separate sixth-form college, and provide education for all 16–19 students, both full-time and part-time. So England's first tertiary college emerged partly through the example of the sixth-form college, which prepared the ground for its acceptance; but partly also because of the success of the FE college in doing the traditional job of the schools. The chickens had finally come home to roost.

The move towards a break at 16

A useful summary of the characteristics of tertiary colleges has been published by the Tertiary College Panel (Janes and Miles, 1978): by 1979 fifteen tertiary colleges had been established. Sixth-form colleges are more numerous, and there are likely to be a hundred of them by 1980. An interesting account of their development, with particular reference to one such college, has been written by Macfarlane (1978). The number of sixth-form and tertiary colleges can be expected to increase in the next few years, particularly by the mid-1980s as the fall-off in the number of tertiary students makes small sixth forms a costly proposition in many areas. Over 10 per cent of full-time 16–19 education is currently carried out in sixth-form or tertiary colleges, and the DES has made no secret of its enthusiasm for these institutions.

There are three aspects to the trend: political, economic and educational. The present confused state of political battle-lines is well illustrated by the inconsistency of attitudes to the separate tertiary institution. It is supported, for example, by such left-of-centre figures as Benn and Simon (1972), and Pedley (1973); but the Conservative 1976 Bow Group pamphlet on education advocates more 11–16 comprehensive schools. Yet the Liberal Party's spokesman on education is reported (*The Times*, 6.9.77) as declaring that the DES 'was discouraging the establishing of sixth forms in some schools, making it impossible for a true comprehensive system to develop'. At the parish pump, parties will tend to take their cue from the views of parents and teachers, particularly if reorganisation is a controversial issue and there is no coherent policy in the authority; and these groups—for different reasons, no doubt—tend to oppose a break at 16. A compromise solution is to make one school the sixth form for a group of schools, so that a 'mushroom' 11–18 school runs alongside a group of 11–16 schools. The political appeal of turning the established grammar school into a mushroom comprehensive is greater for the right than the left, but it is a scheme which has been generally recognised as offering the worst of both worlds (see, for example, Peterson 1973), and which the DES has consistently opposed.

There is really no article of faith which prevents either of the main parties from developing separate tertiary institutions. The Luton council was Labour-controlled in 1966, when the first such institution appeared in the maintained sector; and the Hampshire County Council was Conservative-controlled in 1969, when it adopted a general policy of a break at 16. It is arguable that at the moment neither party has much of an education policy, and that grass-roots forces thus have a proportionately greater effect on how local difficulties are resolved. This is another way of saying that in the absence of the leadership that a well-governed country ought to expect from its politicians, we are passing through a stage when policies are made instead by well-organised pressure groups. The education of no age group can flourish in such a climate. But in the longer term, there is no reason to doubt that, for whatever reasons are expedient or appropriate, more tertiary institutions will appear.

In many cases, economic arguments will ultimately be influential. A cynic, indeed, might argue that in educational decisions, our inability to agree on what constitutes an educational good means that we always prefer to let hard cash make our minds up; that every educational idea has its price, and its day will dawn when the price is right. It is certainly true that even the move to comprehensive reorganisation, which came about on a tide of dissatisfaction with selection that must be the nearest one can get to a national education trend, was generally accompanied by the suggestion that the bipartite system wasted the talent of our children, and that on its development our sustained technological well-being depended. The level of argument tends to be cruder when 16–19 education is involved. The average size of a school sixth form group is 8.0, compared with 12.5 in a sixth-form or tertiary college; and the colleges can offer a far wider range of courses into the bargain. It is a compelling comparison when rate increases threaten.

But it is by no means an open-and-shut case. Schools contrive to offer sixth-form provision for as few as 60 students on an effective staffing ratio of one teacher to 10 or 12 students, and this is the same figure to which the colleges work. There are difficulties in comparing salary costs, and also the costs of providing and maintaining the institutions. Taking sixth formers out of schools leaves classrooms empty which still incur running costs; but it would be different if falling school rolls led to the closure of a whole school, and this is already certain in several areas. There is also the shortage of teachers in some specialisms: is it better to concentrate them in the colleges, or to leave them in the schools, with no colleges to compete for them? Certainly there is a profound shortage of basic data on costs, even on matters like staffing and maintenance costs which can at least be defined in quantitative terms. It seems extraordinary that the DES has no comparative figures of this kind, in spite of the statistics returned every year by schools and LEAs. But even when they are available, it is likely that in a given area, the decision to set up separate tertiary institutions will need some kind of local *coup de grace* to make it stick. The context of falling rolls is bound to offer opportunities.

The educational arguments are therefore far from unimportant. They must take primacy in our own deliberations, and they will have a growing significance in the *realpolitik* of the council chamber. As interest grows in the kind of educational provision needed in the tertiary sector, so will it in the ability of schools and colleges to provide courses in adequate variety. The DES has argued that about 140 is the minimum size for a sixth form to give a wide enough choice of subjects, assuming a not ungenerous staffing ratio of 1 teacher to 10 students and that A-level is the higher-level examination prevailing. The N and F proposals would have stretched school resources to their limit, as the Schools Council's own studies showed. This seems to be inevitable with any two-tier subject-based scheme. So a sixth form of 140 is none too big. We have seen, in the previous chapter, how difficult it is for schools to provide a sound range of sixth form studies with smaller numbers, unless one of five possible courses of action is followed. Either the extra resources must come out of the lower school; or they must be provided (as, for instance, in inaccessible rural areas) as a legitimate bonus by the LEA; or schools must cooperate in their provision for minority subjects; or a local sixth-form centre must be established; or a federated scheme must pool 16–19 provision for an area.

The alternative is a break at 16, and the first issue must then be that of the viability of the 11–16 school. Here again there is a woeful shortage of hard facts, and any detailed discussion of this point lies outside the strict scope of this book. The Secondary Heads Association has, however, published (1979) the results of a questionnaire completed in 1977 by the heads of 170 11–16 schools, and this helps to throw light on some of the assertions often made about the effects on the 11–18 school of removing the sixth form. 77 per cent of heads, for instance, reported that 'they normally recruited staff of high quality and good experience'; honours graduates outnumbered the other staff by about 2:1 (with large local variations); only two schools denied teaching French, and 63 per cent of the heads replying knew of no staff departing in search of sixth form work. 72 per cent of heads thought that 11–16 or 12–16 schools were a satisfactory or acceptable alternative to all-through schools with a sixth form, and the reason chiefly given in support of 11–16 schools was 'the enhanced status, responsibility and leadership of fifth form pupils'. The survey's conclusion that 'the outlook is not, perhaps, as dark as some feared' seems amply justified.

This, then, is one side of the argument for separate 16–19 institutions. We must now consider the styles of education offered by the sixth-form and tertiary college, and see how they compare with the school-based alternatives.

The sixth-form college

It has been noted that the sixth-form college evolved additively from the school sixth form, and does not supplant the FE college. Indeed the fact that it must operate under school rather than FE regulations expressly prevents it from doing so, and the existence of a sixth-form college implies the existence in the area of an FE college which will provide not only courses for adult and part-time students, but also a range of courses for full-time 16–19 students which can only be offered under FE regulations. The tertiary college, on the other hand, is formed not so much by addition as by absorption; its regulations allow it to offer courses of any kind, subject only to the avoidance of course duplication or overlap within a given region. It therefore embraces both school sixth-form work and the normal FE provision.

The staffing of the two kinds of tertiary institution reflects these distinctions. That of the sixth-form college is necessarily drawn, on formation, from the staffs of the comprehensive or grammar schools—usually the latter—from which it is being constructed. And further appointments will be made from the ranks of teachers qualified to perform in schools. But the tertiary college will bring together both school teachers and FE lecturers, the teachers transferring under assured-salary arrangements to the equivalent FE lecturer scale. Most commonly the FE college will be the nucleus of the operation, because it will have the costly technical and craft facilities needed for vocational courses already installed. But the tertiary college must absorb school staff from the sixth forms whose work it takes over, and so an intermingling of staff from two very different traditions is inevitable. This has been so, for example, even in the case of the single tertiary college (Cricklade College, Andover) which has so far been purpose-built. The staff were drawn in part from a former grammar school, and in part by new appointments from both the school and FE sectors.

Few of the sixth-form colleges are more than ten years old, and few of the tertiary colleges more than five. It follows that they are still evolving and adapting, and that there is more variation in practice between the colleges than one would expect to find between, say, school sixth forms of comparable size and facilities. On the other hand, as essentially two-year institutions their input and output parameters are closely defined, and there is scarcely much time between these two student-states to allow for wild and unexpected departures from the norm. It is therefore not too early to gauge the characteristic styles of the two kinds of college, and to identify the issues which give rise to different individual solutions.

The English sixth form was developed by Morant's grammar schools from a public school model, and the comprehensive school has had little scope for varying the basic pattern. University preparation is the core of the work, using the subject-based GCE A-level examination as the curriculum stereotype. One-year sixth formers have been offered a diet mainly of GCE O-levels, and the needs of less conventionally academic students have been met to some extent by extending the choice of exam subjects. Thus A-levels in sociology and engineering science might be found, along with O-levels in, say, computer science or environmental studies so as to make a change from those taken at 16-plus. But these extra subjects are expensive to mount, and since most comprehensive sixth forms are on the small side, the extra resources are hard to come by. The Certificate of Extended Education (CEE) is still without official validation, and is not available in all LEAs. But some schools have seen it as a more satisfactory one-year course than O-level and added it to their programmes.

The sixth-form college has taken over this essentially grammar-school pattern, and in the main its nucleus of staff has been drawn from the same background. Even so, it has had to establish itself in a community probably prejudiced in favour of the smaller sixth form in an all-through school. It is reasonable, then, that the new college would tend to base its structure and style fairly conservatively on what had gone before. But it has one invaluable asset denied to its antecedents: economies of scale give it the resources to expand substantially the range of subjects offered, and so reach out for a wider intake of students. Apart from the territorial instinct, the favourable emphasis given by the Burnham regulations to older students makes expansion as desirable for the sixth-form college as does the FE criterion of student-hours for the tertiary college. But expansion is scarcely possible at the upper end of the ability range, and so sixth-form colleges have gone beyond extra O and A-level subjects to offer CSE, CEE and RSA (Royal Society of Arts) business studies courses in a big way. Then there are the examinations offered by the Institute of Linguists, the London Chamber of Commerce, Pitmans and City and Guilds Foundation courses; along with EFL (English as a foreign language) and pre-nursing courses. The larger comprehensive schools had, as early as the mid-sixties, offered a few of these more vocational courses for students of roughly average ability, usually as odd RSA typing options; but some, remoter from FE colleges and with a sympathetic LEA, had set up very successful sixth-form commercial courses running alongside A and O-levels. The sixth-form college has the resources to extend this vocational emphasis, and thus recruit students of a much wider range of ability than would ever be found in the grammar-school sixth.

These students have had an important effect in loosening up sixth-form college attitudes. In the early seventies one could certainly find colleges with uniform regulations; it would be unusual now. Yet it appears that a fair proportion of schools retain them for their sixth formers. The fact is that if tertiary students are quite separate from younger pupils, they incline to more adult patterns of behaviour and this is reflected in the rules the institution devises for them. The lack of discipline problems in sixth-form and tertiary colleges is commonly remarked upon by college staff with school experience. In sixth forms, it seems as if the presence of younger pupils can have a provocative effect, or simply make it harder for students to shake off younger habits. Adolescents mature more quickly than in Dr Arnold's day; it may be that the role of moral exemplar to the lower school comes more readily to fourth and fifth formers—if appropriately fostered—than to our sixth formers.

In moving their sixth-form centres away from the heart of the school, many schools have responded to this trend. They may even allow sixth formers to opt out of school assemblies, but the 1944 Education Act's requirement of a daily 'act of worship' means that some kind of organised school function in the moral, religious or corporate domain will occur, and the sixth form will not be unaware of it. Even if it chose to, no school can draw a *cordon sanitaire* around its sixth form. The sense of belonging is inescapable.

In a two-year college, on the other hand, a student will not so readily feel part of a wider community. But how far will he want to? The attitude towards assembly is of interest here. Sixth-form colleges tend to retain it, at least once a week: they 'are concerned . . . that their students should identify with the place' (Macfarlane, 1978). It will be a form of shared experience, whether for communicating information, or as an annex to the general studies programme. To some, this may smack of paternalism, reflecting the roots of the colleges in grammar-school sixth forms. To others, it provides institutional support for the student's growth to adulthood. But weekly assemblies are unlikely to be found in tertiary colleges, where 'The centre of student affairs . . . is the students' union' (Janes and Miles, 1978). It would appear, from personal observation, that either approach is perfectly valid: students are adaptable creatures, and seem to be able to find a corporate identity in a variety of ways. Few colleges, though, would be so bold as to claim they had found ways of giving all students social involvement in a two-year institution.

There are some signs that sixth-form colleges are as anxious to cast off the yoke of the grammar-school sixth form as are tertiary colleges that of the FE college. A number of sixth-form colleges, for example, run one-year qualifying or 'foundation' courses specially intended for students with a few low-grade CSEs or even none. These courses represent much curriculum innovation. They may lead to a college certificate, and aim to promote self-reliance and initiative as well as literacy and numeracy. Another variant is described by Macfarlane (1978): a student with a reading age below 11 is given remedial English, along with eight general studies options selected from a wide range of 'main studies', and which are a general-education component of the timetable of all students.

These are enterprising moves, showing ingenuity in adapting a college's courses to meet the requirements of individual students. Traditional FE colleges have been known to show a certain lack of enthusiasm for students with such marginal entry attainments, and the record of grammar schools in coping with their O-level failures is a sorry one. These approaches reflect the care 16–19 colleges take in devising guidance and counselling systems which follow, in essence, the practice of pastoral care developed in comprehensive schools but often executed much more scrappily in the sixth form. A two-tier system of group tutor and senior tutor—corresponding to form tutor and house or year tutor in a school—is usually adopted, and the absence of younger pupils to think about means that the job is done well. And in any case, since nothing is known about the students at first hand, nothing can be taken for granted. The 16–19 college cannot help but devise efficient procedures for linking with its contributory schools, and collating information about each year's fresh intake. It is easy in a school sixth form, on the other hand, to assume that there is nothing new to find out about a student because he has already been around for five years.

The sixth-form college will show the same intensity of purpose in its approach to general studies. Macfarlane declares that 'The seriousness with which the comprehensive colleges (*sic*) have approached the non-examination part of their curriculum has become one of their most distinctive features', and sees this as an important agent for broadening the curriculum:

Whereas the N and F pattern seeks to provide breadth and balance in the student's programme of examination courses, the comprehensive colleges have sought to compensate for the comparative narrowness of the three-examination-subject system by means of an extensive general studies programme and the provision of a variety of other activities.

The sixth-form colleges, in short, have the time and the money to make general studies something more than a good intention gone to seed. The conventional philosophy of balancing specialist study in depth with core study in breadth can be backed by conviction and resources, and made more effective than in many sixth forms. Freedom from the constraints of a main-school timetable means that general studies periods need not be sacrificed in order to fit in, say, the eighth A-level physics period.

There is, however, more to general studies than devising courses on a variety of subjects, grouping them perhaps under general headings, and requiring students to complete their timetables by a selection from the lists. Crowther's distinction between complementary and common studies is still valid, and needs to be considered in comparing general studies schemes with, for example, the N and F proposals for a broader curriculum, or the International Baccalaureate scheme discussed in Chapter 4. My impression is that in determining the individual student's general studies programme, the sixth-form college (and, for that matter, the tertiary college) is likely to pay more attention to the student's personal interests and preferences than to some structured scheme which acknowledges personal interests and career focusing, but which at the same time ensures that experiences are offered in key cultural areas. General studies might even be used to enhance work in examination subjects: Macfarlane (1978) remarks that

> If it is thought that a student very much needs width of experience in a particular subject area he may occasionally take Main Study music or art or science as well as GCE O or A-level in the same subject, the approach of the Main Study being quite different from that of the examination course.

The point about the different approach is crucial; an educative programme, as Richard Pring says in Chapter 2, can depend 'on how one teaches rather than what one teaches'. The term 'main study' is used at Queen Mary's College, Basingstoke to denote a programme of general studies options spread throughout the timetable, and which occupy 7 periods of the time of a three A-level student (each A-level taking 4 periods), or 15 periods of the time of a student taking four CEE subjects; and which, as we have seen, can also form the backbone of a student on a qualifying course. In contrast, 'Core Studies' at Brockenhurst College, Hampshire offers a choice of general and recreational studies under four heads, and occupying one treble period and two double periods weekly in inviolate blocks.

Whatever the preferred arrangement and title given to these minority-time courses, we can be sure that college students cannot avoid them, and may well enjoy them: Macfarlane quotes a survey of ex-students which showed that 60 per cent made a favourable comment on 'Main Studies', 28 per cent were neutral and only 12 per cent unfavourable. The Schools Council's 1970 survey found that while 43 per cent of sixth formers would prefer to spend more time on general studies, the figure for ex-sixth formers was 70 per cent. So the colleges are meeting a need, and can justify a pragmatic balance between what might be good for a student, and what he is likely to take an interest in. But this may not be the same as ensuring a given degree of compensating study, or that a common core of, say, moral, social, aesthetic and philosophical studies is undertaken by all students. Whether or not we agree on the need for these good things, we do need a clear understanding of exactly what really happens in this minority-time curriculum area.

There is much to admire in the verve and industry shown by sixth-form colleges in turning optioned general-studies courses into a going concern. But they seem to have baulked at the task of developing an integrated core of common studies as a part of the minority-time element. The explanation is probably that the colleges have based their appeal on choice—choice of O-level, A-level, CEE and general studies courses. This is extrinsic choice between subjects or course topics, rather than intrinsic choice within a wider curriculum theme. Without doubt, the choice principle is attractive to students, and the sixth-form college can afford to stress it. But it can be overdone; the DES has expressed fears that some colleges may be offering too many different and often overlapping A-levels. It is one thing to add extra languages, crafts and social studies to the basic dozen, and end up with 16 or 20; it is another to offer 27 or more, when 10 subjects provide 80 per cent of all entries. It is possible to spread the teaching effort too thinly.

Set alongside many school sixth forms, the well-run sixth-form college has the sleekness and efficiency of an adaptable hatchback compared with a T-model Ford. Basically, it does the same things; but it can do them superbly well. It is not a new concept—Benn (1978) prefers to talk of the sixth-form college as 'the sixth-form school'—but it has brought new life to an old one. It has extended its range, and softened the grammar-school rigidities with a fresh warmth and understanding. It has found an organic unity which gives its students a committed liveliness: a quality often lacking in school sixth forms, eking out a handful of students in humdrum accommodation with patchy resources. Undoubtedly the school sixth form can be as good as this; but it is equally certain that not many are.

The sixth-form college is really an old dog improving its tricks. Just as the grammar school cannot exist without the secondary modern or creamed comprehensive alongside it to absorb its rejects, so the sixth-form college needs an FE college in its area to cope with the full-time pupils who cannot be adapted to its single-subject examination structures or its firmer pastoral embrace. This will be true of any school sixth form, too, whether selective or comprehensive. But the sixth-form college has shown remarkable resilience in widening its natural market sector. Even so, it can hardly be a 'comprehensive' college, when many other courses are available only at institutions operating under FE regulations. One cannot but wonder whether at least some of the students at a sixth-form college might be better suited to the alternatives that are denied them.

The tertiary college

The tertiary college has had to learn new tricks. This seems surprising, because its nuclear FE segment will already have offered the full range of courses, and the sixth-form college has had to extend the traditional sixth-form range. But the tertiary college has had to integrate two rather different traditions. It cannot absorb the new sixth-form staff and students simply by expanding its A-level business. Although bilateral mergers of this kind are not unknown in the formation of comprehensive schools from grammar and modern schools, tertiary students are young adults and have to be seen in the round. E. King (1976) has written that

> All students at this level are in a real sense 'new' . . . supposed difficulties in considering many young adult needs generically arise from the institutionalisation of courses, credentials and the teaching professions in their variety. They are problems of demarcation, not real educational problems.

And in any case, lines of demarcation are scarcely likely to appeal to the school and FE staff brought together in the new single institution. It is clear, too, that the paternalism of the school sixth form cannot be reserved for one group of students, and the remoter character of the FE college set aside for the other. There has to be a common, consistent policy. In hammering it out both school and FE patterns will contribute, but each will need to change.

Neither pattern is without its faults. The drift from school to college in the 1960s, and the comments revealed by Fogelman's study and mentioned in the previous chapter, show that not only have schools responded slowly to the changing social and cultural identities of tertiary students; they have skimped on career guidance and breadth of study. Yet they have a tradition of care, of a close and easy link between tutor and student, which at its best derives from and extends into the quality of teaching; and this is a valuable element. In comparison, the standard FE college of the 1960s was rather a soulless place, and certainly a joyless one. The colleges expanded through the exertions of their heads of departments. Local employers were vigorously canvassed, and part-time courses mounted to meet their needs.

The college was a strictly functional place with a manifest vocational bias, and departments vied with each other for the students on whom growth (and salaries) depended. The principal often found himself a peacemaker, and the robber-baron tradition of the FE department generated its own kind of paternalism. The advent of liberal studies was accepted uneasily, but the growth of A-level courses brought a new respectability. Primitive tutorial systems came into being, the main guidance effort being adequately linked with the vocational departments. To renegades from the sixth form there was a refreshing freedom to go your own way. There were ground rules, but they derived from operational rather than emotional considerations.

One could say that the prime task of the tertiary college is to unite the caring tradition of the school with the respect for the independence of the individual that has been a feature of the FE college. The young adult needs a more supportive advice system than many FE colleges have developed, but a less intrusive context than that of the school sixth form. The tertiary colleges have recognised that the key point here is the linkage between the three-cornered system of student, pastoral tutor and academic course. In particular, the FE tradition of the omnipotent head of department will need to give ground to a tutorial structure. The importance of striking out in a fresh direction from the FE college has been stressed by Janes (1979), writing as a founder-principal of a tertiary college:

> The tertiary college is—or should be—a distinctive new species of 16-plus institution. It should not be the technical college with an added number of full-time A-level students . . . If reorganisation is carried out in a manner which in effect attaches a sixth-form college to a technical college the product is a bilateral, not a comprehensive, and the potential of a tertiary college is largely lost.

Different colleges will adopt different stratagems, depending on local conditions. If the new tertiary college inherits an FE institution with a dominant departmental tradition, the administrative structure may need to show explicitly that the power has shifted. But if there is a strong representation of school staff, then a milder gesture may be sufficient to bring about the desired change of emphasis. The common aim will be to develop interdisciplinary approaches, centralise pastoral functions and reinforce academic planning and its associated support services. Of the 15 tertiary colleges at present in operation, 'eleven have either abandoned the departmental pattern altogether, or have modified it in significant ways' (Janes and Miles 1978). All have taken steps to ensure that a full counselling service is available to incoming students. In some colleges, student admissions are centrally controlled: thus Bridgwater College has a coordinator of student services with head of department status, who is responsible for links with the contributory 11–16 schools, student admissions and the pastoral and support services. In others, such as Yeovil College, the 'deans' link directly with students for the general oversight of pastoral matters, while the subject tutors link with students to ensure that the pattern of individual subjects and options crosses departmental boundaries. This 'matrix' system ensures a separation of pastoral and academic networks, but the same effect can be achieved in other ways. The size of the college will be another determining factor.

The important point is that the tertiary college must, because of its dual origins, seek forms of integration and coherence, and the pastoral system is the right place to start. This will be reinforced in the academic system, since the rather inflexible department-centred FE approach will give way to coordination and mutual servicing. At Cricklade College, for example, 'The Science and Technology Department has no mathematicians of its own . . . the Mathematics Department provides the necessary teaching. . . There are no General Studies lecturers either . . . Almost all lecturers contribute to this programme' (Holman 1977). There is no doubt that these innovations in curriculum and organisation are essential to the development of tertiary colleges, and will in turn have their effect on traditional patterns in FE colleges. In some ways, the distinctions between the tertiary and FE colleges are more significant than between the tertiary and sixth-form colleges, and have come in for less attention than they merit.

Appendix B gives an outline of the courses and structures of Exeter College, which was the first tertiary college and, with over 1600 full-time students, is still the biggest. The average figure is just over 700, compared with nearly 600 for the average sixth-form college. In addition to all the examination courses (except, usually, CEE courses) offered by the sixth-form college, the tertiary college runs a major programme of courses with vocational titles, and which generally constitute a complete curriculum programme. It is easy, too, in a book which attempts to examine curriculum arrangements common to more than one type of institution, to overlook the very substantial commitment of the tertiary college to part-time and maturer adult students. As well as Exeter College's 1650 full-time students, there are, for example, 3000 part-time day students and 2500 attending evening classes.

Of the full-time courses with a vocational theme offered in a tertiary college, the most demanding are Ordinary National Diploma (OND) courses, which have a four O-level entry requirement and are acceptable for university entry. Although academically equivalent to A-level, they have a quite different approach, and it is possible for students in tertiary colleges to change from one to the other. The point is that while an OND in business studies will tackle commerce, accounting and economics, it will also include maths, English and a liberal studies component. Thus the student's inclination and interest is met, and broader but related elements are presented in a coherent fashion. It is difficult to see that such a programme is more vocational than, say, three A-levels in Economics, sociology and maths: and it could well be regarded as having a greater negotiable value if the A-level student did not end up at university—and we must remember that a considerable proportion do not. At the same time, we can see that A-levels better meet the needs of students with the potential scholar's interest in a closely defined field.

For less able students, the Certificate of Office Studies and City and Guilds craft courses compete directly with the CEE market, and seem to have more appeal. An inquiry by the *Times Educational Supplement* (15.7.77) showed that only a quarter of the tertiary colleges ran CEE courses, and one reported no takers. The fact is that a student on a hairdressing course, for instance, would study art and retail management as well as the more obvious subjects, and thus continue to develop both basic and commercially useful skills which to some extent transcend its vocational orientation. The same can be said of City and Guilds Foundation courses, and the combination of breadth of appeal with breadth of study is an aspect of other secretarial and foundation courses. Modular course structures and options systems make it possible to combine GCE O and A-levels with vocational courses or modules; thus a two-year advanced secretarial course might combine Pitman's secretarial elements with one or two A-levels, and an English A-level set might contain not only conventional academic students, but also adults on part-time courses as well as other full-time students engaged primarily on vocational courses.

Developments of this kind suggest that the criticism of tertiary colleges as essentially non-integrated FE courses alongside O and A-levels is wide of the mark. But the inverse argument is sometimes encountered: if the college has achieved integration, then the adult and part-time students will make it amorphous, lacking a corporate spirit. The only effective counter to this is to visit a tertiary college and talk to the students. But three general points are worth making. First, the stereotypes don't run true: the dewy-eyed freshness of academic 16 year olds is not tainted by the worldliness of the part-timers, nor undermined by the painstaking plod of adults. Second, there would seem to be much to be said for regarding the tertiary sector as a capital opportunity to lead the adolescent from the protective security of the schoolroom to the world of career and commerce, and the presence of part-time and adult students alongside full-time 16–19 students looks like an eminently sensible way of doing it. One can have too much of a good thing: corporate spirit can become the cloying closeness of the private society. Third, the tertiary college—through its vocational courses and business connexions—sees learning not only for its own sake, but also as something that can be usefully applied. Whitehead's remark that 'Education is the acquisition of the art of the utilisation of knowledge' has never really sunk into the traditional grammar-school view of culture, and this country's extraordinary neglect of the practical arts of the engineer might be remedied if our academic students could see the distinction between pure and applied knowledge for the sham it is. It is worth adding that on average, two-thirds or more of the staff in a tertiary college have industrial or professional experience, and many will have current consultancy, research or professional practice.

Schools and colleges

A more searching criticism might be that all this is very well, but what matters ultimately is the quality of study; and certainly for the more academic student, there is a risk that this might be less in evidence when a class of students does not share a common interest in the pursuit of scholarship. The argument implies that the Crowther concept of 'intellectual discipleship' could certainly flourish in a school sixth form, and possibly in a sixth-form college: but hardly in a tertiary college. Dean and Choppin (1977), for example, quote a working party of the National Association of Divisional Executives: 'courses in colleges of further education are rarely geared to the academic standards provided at present in the sixth form of grammar schools.' Now that 80 per cent of our pupils are in comprehensive schools, this 1970 comment has a dated look to it. And it is interesting that some research by H B Miles (1979), comparing the A-level scores of students in grammar and comprehensive schools, showed that the type of school had a negligible effect on A-level performance: 'Other factors, perhaps many in number, difficult to identify and measure, were responsible for more than half the observed differences in performance'. So we must not too readily assume that academic traditions guarantee high standards, or are incapable of transfer to new kinds of institution.

Whether we call it study in depth, academic rigour or intellectual discipleship, learning should be a high-quality two-way process. The teacher seeks to initiate the student into a world of understanding and imagination, and the student will be encouraged to question and discuss. And these should be the characteristics not only of academic or A-level learning, but of all learning. They are as important to an understanding of Palmerston's foreign policy as they are to the design of burglar alarms. And no institution has a monopoly of them. The pressure for good A-level grades can force the most scholarly sixth-form teacher to make exam tricks and set notes as prominent as Socratic dialogue. The ex-technical college lecturer may stand as close to his overhead projector as he once did to his blackboard, even though he may now be part of a tertiary college. Any 16–19 institution must be vigilant in the pursuit of learning quality, and if we accept Crowther's suggestion that good practice will be found in the schools, then it is as likely to transfer to the tertiary as to the sixth-form college.

It was suggested in Chapter 5 that two other dimensions of 16–19 education, as well as quality of study, are curriculum breadth and the interactions of students with themselves, with the wider community and perhaps with younger pupils. Let us take the interactive aspect first. It is clear that if there is a break at 16, there will be fewer opportunities for tertiary students to influence secondary pupils, and possibly none at all. But both sixth-form and tertiary colleges encourage students to retain their ties, if they wish, with their former schools. School-college liaison is part of the system, and schools can take the initiative by inviting former pupils to join in music and drama productions, as well as assisting with games and expeditions. Most colleges also foster community links, from service projects to fund-raising schemes. Within the college, students will stage productions and write magazines, as in a sixth form; but it is likely that they will have a bigger influence on how the place is run than is usual in a school. The sixth-form college will have some kind of council or committee with its own consultative procedure, depending on the inclinations of the principal. The tertiary college has a more specific mechanism: the Weaver Report led to Circular 7/70, which specifies the broad representation of governing bodies under further and higher education regulations, and gives them considerable autonomy. The academic board gives elected members of the teaching staff an active role in decision-making, and student representation on the governing body ensures that students have a defined role in the tertiary college. Furthermore, the tertiary college will have its student union and its union fund, with further scope for student involvement.

It is notoriously difficult to get the checks and balances right in participatory schemes that carry legislative force. Apathy might reinforce a hierarchy, or open the door to the cabals of political activists. Given the short residence time of the students, the latter danger is more likely to come from the staff. The safeguard here must be the sensitivity and alertness of senior staff, and the growth of a tradition of keen and perceptive corporate involvement. It looks as if the tertiary colleges have taken the provisions of Circular 7/70 in their stride, even though the procedure for suspending, for instance, a student guilty of a breach of discipline is of such Byzantine complexity that he might have finished his course before the outcome is settled. But provisions of this kind have become an aspect of industrial life in the seventies, and seeing how they work at first hand is arguably a part of a student's political education. In contrast, the sixth-form college operates under school regulations and student participation is a grace-and-favour matter. Even so, some mechanism for taking student views into account is bound to exist.

The curriculum possibilities of the tertiary college are particularly interesting, and although they have been exploited to some extent, their potential is considerable. They stem from the opportunities they offer to combine curriculum breadth with an individual theme, interest or vocation. They are lacking from the sixth-form college, because the single-subject basis of CSE, CEE, O and A-level (and N and F-levels) greatly restricts the developer's scope. The single-subject exam is a worked-out seam: it promotes an over-specialised course, which can be offset either by offering more subjects—as in the N and F proposals—or by a counterweight of general studies. The former is of little value unless backed by a prescriptive format, and it necessitates a complex two-tier structure. The latter, even when well done, are inevitably seen as an appendage to the main business of getting good exam results. The final solution to this subject-based line of development is the International Baccalaureate type of approach, which does at least present a coherent curriculum with an attractive combination of optioned and mandatory components.

It is, of course, true that for A-level students, the tertiary college is in the same boat as the sixth-form college, and must devise a general education programme to run alongside the examined subjects. And whereas the sixth-form colleges have gone to much trouble to elaborate on school general-studies schemes and produce a wide choice of well-planned options, the tertiary colleges have adapted both school schemes and the liberal studies programmes which grew up in FE colleges during the sixties to offset some of the more heavily vocational courses. Some tertiary colleges have given careful thought to general studies provision: Exeter College, for example (Appendix B) links them with its pastoral system. But while sixth-form colleges have made a positive feature of general studies, the tertiary colleges seem on the whole to provide more modest schemes. The basic difficulty with all of them, whether in school or college, is that they are a bolt-on extra rather than an integral element. Only if such programmes can be made central to the student's whole curriculum can they generate the engagement on which the process of education depends. Extending the general education of tertiary students is not a matter of applying doses of extraneous knowledge, but of developing his understanding of himself and his cultural inheritance by relating it intimately to his present concerns and future ambitions. And although attempts have been made to put general studies at the centre of the sixth-form programme and A-levels at the periphery (see, for example, Lack 1967), the brutal arithmetic of A-level scores reverses the priority for staff and students alike. Hence the value of whole-curriculum schemes which put breadth and depth in the same package.

The particular virtue of the tertiary college is not only that it brings all tertiary students together, and so presents the opportunity to see these students as a continuum. It also, because of its familiarity with composite courses at a wide range of abilities, has the capacity and resource to develop a portfolio of courses across the ability range which can meet all interests and skills, and at the same time incorporate important elements of general education. In this way, the individual needs of students can be matched to appropriate courses without drawing rigid lines of demarcation, and a breadth of study can be sustained which will be as valuable for the shop assistant as for the Oxbridge scholar. This would presuppose an extensive degree of coordination between departments and courses: but the cross-disciplinary nature of courses like the Certificate of Office Studies or BEC General, for example, requires tertiary colleges to develop linking machinery of this kind. And because of their origins in both school and further education, they are not strangers to the task of devising new curricular patterns and new organisations to match.

Research confirmation that alternatives to the school sixth form are attractive to students and of educational merit comes from an interesting NFER study (Dean, Bradley, Choppin and Vincent 1979). The project followed a sample of 4500 students through forty-five 16–19 institutions: school sixth forms, colleges of FE, sixth-form colleges and tertiary colleges. The students were mainly taking full-time A-level courses, but some were studying for O-levels, ONDs, secretarial qualifications and other FE qualifications. Each student completed a questionnaire in the first term, and another in the final term of the two-year course. It emerged that students were strongly in favour of a college system. Two-thirds felt it was better to be educated in colleges; only 21 per cent opted for schools. Over 80 per cent of those with experience of colleges preferred them:

> It appears that the nature of the educational experience offered by colleges is more often attuned to the mood of today's 16 to 19 years olds than school sixth forms—particularly those operated along traditional lines.

There appeared to be some relationship between the type of 16–19 provision and examination performance, although this was thought to have more to do with differences in the ability of students entering the various institutions than with differences in teaching quality. The mean numbers of A-level passes per student were: grammar sixth form 2.20; tertiary college 2.10; sixth-form college 1.92; comprehensive sixth form 1.88; FE college 1.66. There was also some evidence that tertiary college students with six or less O-levels do better at A-level than similarly qualified students in other institutions. The researchers felt that the limited range of courses offered by sixth-form colleges tended to perpetuate an inappropriate 16-plus division between academic and vocational work, and considered that the tertiary college points the way to the future since it can view post-16 education as a cohesive whole. It should be noted, too, that the study revealed no support for the various arguments against a break at sixteen, on the grounds that this will deter students from working-class backgrounds from staying on:

> We could find no evidence to support this. While students whose fathers are in manual occupations are under-represented in post-compulsory education in general, they are not particularly under-represented in the 16–19 colleges.

We can expect to see an increasing degree of development in tertiary colleges as these very young institutions become both more numerous and more experienced. With the whole range of OND, BEC, TEC, CGLI and A-level courses at its disposal, the tertiary college commands a complete kit of curriculum parts. The sixth-form colleges have little in prospect but the official recognition of CEE. Without this examination, their scope for adapting average students to single-subject courses is greatly curtailed. Some have also identified problems which N and F would have created for their sophisticated minority-time structures—an unkind cut from which they have been spared. As things stand, the sixth-form college is an admirable machine which has reached its ultimate state of development: it cannot escape its genetic origin in the school sixth form and the single-subject examination. But the tertiary college is only at the beginning of its development, and it offers a unique chance to bring unity and coherence to tertiary education.

For the sixth-form college, the way ahead must be to steal some of the tertiary college's clothes; in particular, to have the freedom to mount the course-based programmes with a vocational flavour which, at the moment, are only permissible under FE regulations. If the absurd division between school and FE regulations were eased or bridged, then both schools and sixth-form colleges might gain a new lease of life. But the two territories have been carefully staked out, and it would need resolute political will to abolish the frontier entirely. But compromise is possible. Schools and sixth-form colleges might be licensed to mount certain BEC and TEC courses, taking account of local provision and proximity to FE colleges. Some relaxation might be allowed in the matter of teacher qualifications, permitting unqualified technical staff to teach on approved courses only under school regulations.

To any rational outsider, the separate existence of two different kinds of 16–19 institution can only be the result of some absurd accident. And so, indeed, it is; but the accident of separating academic from technical education happened a long way back, and these things take time. It is just that in the context of our present industrial society and its uncertain future, the binary division looks more and more nonsensical as each day passes.

Economic logic dictates that the two sectors must move closer together, quite apart from the educational case that has been made here for extending further the curriculum potential of the tertiary college. It is likely, though, that for some time yet we shall continue to see more new sixth-form than tertiary colleges established, simply because the sixth-form college is that much closer to the school, and therefore more acceptable to local councillors, teachers and parents when falling rolls oblige LEAs to take action over diminishing schools and their sixth forms. But in the longer run—once the hurdle of a break at 16 has been jumped—the tertiary college solution is bound to become more widespread. It is significant, for example, that in 1979 the Conservative-controlled London borough of Richmond-upon-Thames replaced two sixth-form colleges—set up in 1973 when the borough went comprehensive with 11–16 schools—and a college of technology with a single tertiary college. Despite one of the country's highest rates of post-16 transfer to full-time education, falling rolls had pointed to the tertiary college as the only viable answer.

In educational terms the two traditions have much to learn from each other. The sixth-form college can contribute a sensitive understanding of the role of corporate coherence in supporting students, pioneering work in one-year foundation courses, and imaginative and successful teaching of the A-level plus general studies course. The tertiary college has developed flexible pastoral and academic management systems, a respect for student autonomy and a range of courses which use subject specialisms not as separate examined components but as part of whole-curriculum pro-grammes which associate a study focus with a broader background of experiences. As the 11–16 comprehensive school moves towards a common curriculum, so the tertiary college becomes the logical 16–19 institution.

7
Modular Courses and New Strategies

We must now look at 16–19 education in the light of the preceding analysis and discussion, and see what new departures might profitably be made. Despite the variety of students' needs and talents, and of the institutions and courses seeking to cope with them, two themes constantly recur: first, that of *general education* to equip the student with a foundation for personal adaptation and continuing study, and second, *directed education* which takes account of his current needs and interests. And while one course might emphasize the first element, and another the second, we recognise that both elements will always be present, and will interact to a greater or lesser extent depending upon how a course is put together. For even the most narrowly directed course of training must involve some integration with other subjects—the mechanical skill of typing cannot be sensibly separated from those of layout and language use. And no programme of general education can fail to make a student more aware of the range of specific activities which contribute to our society and culture.

A unifying view

The first essential, therefore, as Richard Pring has pointed out in Chapter 2, is to see the contrast 'not between education and training, but between narrow and educative approaches to the training programme'. And if we can make general education a part of directed education, we have at the same time resolved the issue of depth versus breadth; to say that the particular directed focus of the programme must be put in a broader perspective is to accept the interdependence of depth and breadth. Finally, we define curriculum balance by making up our minds about the nature of this interdependence.

The solution to tertiary education problems, then, turns on integrating general, technical and vocational education within a coordinated programme. The OECD study *Beyond Compulsory Schooling* accepts this as a clear trend in 16–19 education, pointing out that:

> Such a trend invalidates a number of assumptions, such as that of a radical opposition between general and vocational education or the existence of two

types of ability ('academic-theoretical' and 'practical-vocational') warranting a division between intellectual and manual tasks with a wide scale of values and degrees of prestige.

It also invalidates the convenient assumption that the best way to organise a tertiary programme is to add together a range of separate subject components, each independently defined and assessed. For if we accept that directed education and general education are to be organically linked, then we must look at the overall shape of the programme first and its component parts second. We are talking—to quote Pring in Chapter 2 again—about 'the distinction between an education consisting in a group of subject courses and an education consisting in a course that integrates a number of subjects'. It is indeed 'a crucial distinction' because until we make it, we cannot escape from an additive view of the tertiary curriculum: one that is no more than the sum of its separate subject parts. And the integrative approach can, as Pring remarks, be adopted 'at any level from that of the one-year pre-apprenticeship course to A-level'. What will change will be the nature of the integrating element, depending on what we want the course to do.

What we are in effect doing is changing the way in which we look at knowledge. We are not denying the value or usefulness of organising it into subjects, but suggesting that when it comes to designing courses, our primary choice of educational experiences may need to take account of other ways of looking at it. Which other way we choose will depend partly on our personal beliefs and partly on the scope of the course. Different opinions are held as to how knowledge is put together, and some might be more appropriate for a given purpose than others. In this, as in most educational issues, value judgments must be made.

We might, for example, take the view that knowledge can be characterised into a number of distinct 'forms of understanding' (Hirst 1965) or 'realms of meaning' (Phenix 1974). If our planned course is to cover the whole sweep of knowledge, then we might decide to organise it with these as the basis. Such an approach is outlined by Richard Whitfield in Chapter 4, using six groups of 'meanings'. Pring, on the other hand, eschews this approach (Chapter 2) in favour of one which recognises distinctive elements—he quotes the 'philosophical, historical and social aspects of science'—but keeps the focus of the course as the generalising theme. In emphasising how we teach, rather than what we teach, Pring sees the wider perspective emerging from different ways of looking at the focusing theme rather than different and disparate segments of knowledge.

And yet, what is perhaps surprising is not the difference between these points of view, but their similarity when applied to the tertiary sector. For

Whitfield stresses the way in which the distinct kinds of meanings interact between his suggested faculty structure, and the need for a 'differential time allocation' between the meanings or 'modes of consciousness', to take account of 'students' abilities, motivation and likely career aspirations'. Despite different basic premisses, the common result is the notion of a tertiary curriculum which brings general and directed forms of education together in a unified whole. A study of pre-university education in five countries—France, West Germany, Sweden, USA and USSR—by Hearnden (1973) reaches a similar conclusion:

> As far as the curriculum is concerned, the conflict is between the claims of a broad curriculum and those of a depth of study in the subjects in which the primary interests of sixth formers may lie. In the countries studied in this survey the attempt to resolve the conflict is in every case by means of a common core of studies. This is seen not just as a way of combating over-specialisation but in a much more positive sense as representing a unity, the indispensable components of the culture to be transmitted at the upper secondary level.

There are dangers, though, in making too sharp a distinction between the common core and the specialist course components. The notion of a unified course can easily be lost—as, indeed, it usually is in the general-studies plus A-levels pattern.

It is difficult to see how tertiary education, in a society which will put a premium on personal autonomy and adaptation, can move in any direction other than towards a synthesis between the general and directed components of education. It is helpful to relate this to the shape of secondary education, partly to see a change of emphasis, and partly because the tertiary student owes so much—or so little—to his secondary years. There are important implications for the 11–16 curriculum and I have examined these in some detail elsewhere (Holt 1979). For the present, we can see that the task of compulsory schooling must be to offer to all pupils educational experiences which introduce him to key aspects of our culture. Without a map of the culture, he will be ill-prepared for either tertiary education or the world of paid work and increasing leisure. And while a common 11–16 curriculum will always take account of individual interest and purpose in the way in which its learning experiences are organised, and in the 14–16 years by allowing an optioned component, its essential task is to devise a programme of general education which can reach out and touch every pupil.

And the tertiary sector, too, will be very much in the business of general education. But there is a shift in emphasis. In secondary education, the unifying theme is to mediate the culture, by a process of negotiation that will absorb the skills and resources of the teacher in each area of knowledge and understanding. In tertiary education, the unifying theme will be the guiding interest or purpose of the student's course of study. General education is then not a detached package, separate from directed education; it is a permeating influence. The analogy is with a fruit cake rather than a doughnut.

Moves towards coherence

How is such a course to be organised? A useful starting point is the attempt, set out in Schools Council *Working Paper 45* (1972), to broaden the A-level curriculum. Looking at this simply as a design exercise, we can see how good intentions went astray. It seems clear that the original idea was to make breadth an organic part of the programme, as is argued here. The value of an integrative structure other than conventional subjects was appreciated, and eight 'elements of a balanced curriculum' were listed. These constituted the model for the broader curriculum pattern, and resulted from the Second Sixth Form Working Party's having 'carefully considered the elements necessary for breadth and balance in the sixth form curriculum'. The model, in other words, was derived from some rationale of the whole curriculum. The next step was to convert it into organised learning experiences, and here again the committee saw that an integrative format could be used. But 'For most teachers . . . these things are still in the future. They have been brought up in their subjects and they think in subject terms'. So subjects it was, and a spread of five was deemed to be necessary. But even if the choice of these showed 'balance'—and the requirement was purely advisory—it would still be necessary to provide general studies for nearly 30 per cent of the time, for the job of 'integrating the separate subjects or their subject perspectives'.

The three critical steps in this reasoning are these. First, the choice of rationale used in substantiating the model: second, the choice of separate subject components to implement it: and third, the lack of any code of practice to enforce the chosen model. In the event, as we have seen, the failure of the final scheme to win friends and influence people stems from its falling between two stools. Those who seek breadth are dissatisfied by the lack of any guarantee that it will happen, and those who seek specialist skills dislike the five-subject spread, despite the invention of the higher F-level tier. Three further reasons for the scheme's ultimate demise are not of direct concern to us at this moment, but perhaps should be stated: first, doubts about the resource requirements to make N and F work; second, the unfortunate timing of the operation, which would mean the introduction of the new scheme in the mid-eighties, at about the same time as the new General Certificate of Secondary Education (GCSE) might replace O-level and CSE; and last, the current political reaction (which is not confined to these shores) against educational change in any direction other than backwards.

If we now compare the N and F scheme with the International Baccalaureate, we can see how close it comes to a successful formula. Taking the three critical steps again, we see that—first—the IB model of curriculum breadth is also based on a rationale of general education (see, for example, Peterson 1973). Second, it organises the learning under subject headings, with three at higher and three at subsidiary level (see Chapter 4). But the IB does not lose its nerve at the third step: satisfactory performance is stipulated in all six subject areas, and the whole curriculum time available is finally filled by creative, aesthetic and social activities on the one hand, and a common—and plainly integrative—course in the 'theory of knowledge' on the other.

The parallels are close, and it is rather remarkable that after so much labouring in the A-level vineyard, the Schools Council's best solution turns out to be an IB look-alike. But perhaps it is not so remarkable; it could be argued that the IB is the best one can do if the aim is to combine breadth and depth while retaining a separate subject structure. But it needs three essential devices: first, a two-tier structure; second, a properly worked-out and prescribed general studies component; and third: a prescribed format which fills the whole curriculum. And we must remember that the IB is essentially a scheme for university entrance, designed to cater for the ablest segment of the two-year sixth-form population. Indeed, it is difficult to see how an IB-type scheme can be made flexible enough to cater for less convergently academic students, in the way in which A-levels, for example, are currently used in order to broaden the scope of a fundamentally academic examination. Not that A-levels are notably successful at this; but the point is that the IB must be even less so, since it makes demands across a student's whole intellectual spectrum. And this is surely the reason why *Working Paper 45* faltered when it came to laying down the law about exactly how the student should use his time. The Schools Council required a scheme not just for three A-level students, but one which would suit a wider academic range. It could be argued that the N and F scheme failed because it did not go far enough; but if it had gone the whole way and followed the IB, it could not have satisfied its brief. One can see why Dean and Choppin (1977) concluded that:

> The choice therefore seems to be between introducing some system, such as the International Baccalaureate, which ensures the fulfilment of its objectives by covering the entire timetable with a complete spectrum of subjects, and the retention of A-level, perhaps with the adoption of a more positive approach to general studies.

But the prospect of souped-up general studies is not one to set pulses racing, even if married to improved and streamlined A-levels. The Schools Council's N and F subject steering groups ironed out some of the remarkable variations between the examining boards in A-level content for a given subject, and this may well prove to be the chief educational benefit of the whole exercise. But whatever the A-level programme, the separation between general and directed education is retained, and there is no model of curriculum breadth to articulate the components. If we are to stick to schemes which make use of subjects in their own right, then the IB has much to commend it. But if, on the other hand, we turn to schemes which use subjects in terms of the contribution they can make to some course-wide integrating theme, then we break through to a new range of possibilities. We have already noted that a number of further-education courses are constructed in this way. It is now appropriate to look at these approaches in greater detail.

The scope of modular courses

The main difference between a subject-based and a course-based programme will be that the shape and size of the specialist contributions—which may be under a subject heading, or a topic heading—will be subordinate to the unifying, focusing element, rather than autonomous components. It follows that a number of such contributions may be needed, and possibly at different stages in a given course. The total course will therefore be a *modular structure*, made up of a number of distinct units or modules. The modules may or may not correspond to conventional subjects. The point is that, taken as a whole, the pattern of the modules which makes up the course will reflect whatever model is taken as the theme or rationale of the course.

A good example of a simple modular structure which reveals the flexibility of such an arrangement is that for a degree with the Open University (OU). An ordinary degree needs six credits, and you obtain credits by taking courses. A course may be worth a half-credit or a full-credit—the latter simply taking twice the time of the former, at the same level of study. You must start by taking one or two foundation courses, each worth a full-credit. You then take further courses at a higher level, at a maximum rate of two full-credit or four half-credit courses a year. An honours degree needs eight credits, of which at least two must be at third or fourth level. Thus a student might follow the arts foundation course, and the foundation course 'making sense of society', by a series of second-level courses which reflect his interest in the arts/social studies area, but also his changing preference as he decides, perhaps, on a particular topic for third-level honours-degree work. And it should be noted that within a given course, a unit structure may be used: for example, the arts foundation course (Open University 1978) offers 'A series of blocks of work, each centred on a single discipline but demonstrating interrelationships of ideas and methodologies with other disciplines', leading up to 'a large interdisciplinary block in which the concepts and techniques developed are used to study a complex topic.'

In this example, the course theme is the student's own area of interest: he is free to select more or less as he wishes (there is some overlap between certain courses, giving rise to a few restrictions). Note, though, that each foundation course ranges widely: the arts course includes the uses and abuses of argument; history; literature; music; philosophy; art; and religion. As a contrast, consider the BEC General Diploma course for careers in 'business, distribution and the public sector'. This is a one-year full-time course 'for young people in the 16–19 age group with few, if any academic qualifications who expect to enter, or have recently entered, employment' (Business Education Council, 1977). It might well be taken at an FE or tertiary college immediately post-16, and it is meant to supplant the Certificate of Office Studies and other similar courses. Four 'central themes' are identified: money; people; the ability to receive and understand information and to express oneself clearly; and a logical and numerate approach to business problems.

The BEC General Diploma course is made up of eight modules, of two distinct types. Each student must complete three *core modules*, designed to develop 'the basic knowledge, understanding and skills necessary for all students'; the remaining five *option modules* may be chosen by the student from an extensive list, and 'build on the knowledge and understanding established throughout the core'. Sample option modules are: community studies; government; basic elements of travel and tourism; and receptionist/telephonist. The three core modules deal with people and communication, business calculations, and the world of work. The aims of the first core module are concerned with understanding and using language; contributing 'to the student's personal development' through improved communication skills; and integrating communication skills 'to improve the student's effectiveness at work'. A number of 'general objectives' are specified, such as the ability, at the end of the course, to 'write accurately and concisely'. This general objective gives rise to three 'learning objectives': these deal with punctuation and spelling, writing down one's own ideas clearly, and checking and revising work. In this way, a total of 27 learning objectives are specified and these determine the learning experiences for this particular core module.

The BEC National Diploma course is set at a higher level. It is intended to replace the OND business studies courses, and twelve modules must be satisfactorily completed. The four common-core modules cover people and communication; numeracy and accounting; and the organisation in its environment. The latter topic is a double module, including work on organisations in a mixed economy; problems arising from scarcity of resources; demand and supply mechanisms; domestic influences affecting government policies; forms of legal liability, and so on. Then the focus narrows to *board core modules*, named after the subsidiary BEC Boards dealing with business studies, financial sector studies and distribution studies. These modules are directed to 'a more specific range of careers'. Two of these must be chosen, depending on a career interest in accounting, administration, distribution or other fields. Finally, six option modules complete the course, and these generally deal as before with more specialised work. They include such diverse interests as computer studies; insurance; transport; display; and economic history.

A number of points should be noted. First, it is easy to allow for part-time students, and a number of authorities consider these will grow in number in the next few years. For example, the BEC general diploma may either be taken as eight modules in one year, or four in each of two years, with the three core modules in the first year. Second, it is easy to incorporate intermediate levels. With the BEC general course, a part-time student who takes four modules in one year qualifies for a certificate at the end of it; he may then, of course, go on for a second year to the diploma. Flexible devices of this kind are of the first importance in the tertiary sector, where students may have so many different backgrounds and circumstances, and where these can change so rapidly. Third, assessment includes both assignments and an examination for each module, incorporating the element of course-work assessment so significantly missing from Mode 1 O-level and CEE examinations. And finally, all students must undertake *cross-modular assignments*, which integrate the knowledge and understanding acquired in the separate core modules, develop the student's ability to tackle problems systematically, and 'provide a focus around which the course team can integrate the course as a whole'. For example, a student on the full-time one-year BEC general diploma course must spend a minimum of sixty hours' class time on cross-modular assignments.

There is no problem in incorporating sandwich elements of practical work within modular courses, and the credit-accumulation principle not only helps students, but can give modules a wider currency and so sustain their viability. A further illustration of the adaptability of unit-based schemes has been given in a pamphlet (*E/9250/18/2*) produced by the CGLI and describing a number of different ways in which City and Guilds foundation courses can be built into the school curriculum. For one thing, there are a number of areas of study common to the various published courses (Chapter 2): communication studies, optional activities and guidance education are common to all, community and social services to several of them, and so on. So two courses like community care and distribution can be operated together with a large common core, and in another scheme, six courses—community care, engineering, science industries, agriculture, commercial studies and art and design—run in the lower sixth alongside O and A-level courses, with the possibility of some overlap with O-level mathematics and English, and a number of foundation course elements in common.

It is a curious fact that work on modular courses seems to have been carried out in further and higher education, but scarcely at all in schools. The Open University has been a pioneer here, and the Council for National Academic Awards (CNAA) has been active in validating some enterprising schemes. Oxford Polytechnic, for instance, offers a CNAA modular degree course in 25 diverse academic subjects, with a combination of 2 foundation and 21 specialist modules, and which can be taken either full-time over three years or part-time over seven. The CNAA has published a valuable paper (CNAA 1974) which analyses its experience with modular courses and suggests important aspects of their design. It distinguishes the main features of modular courses, which the above examples have illustrated, and identifies flexibility as the main aim. The advantages are that courses can be student-centred; can allow for changing areas of study; can 'encompass both broad and specialised programmes'; can enhance student motivation; and help him understand his goals as part of the process of module selection. But students will need 'much more academic guidance than in conventional courses', and the group of students taking a given module will have a variety of backgrounds and attainments. Timetabling can be awkward unless careful thought is given to module structure. Assessment needs to take into account comparability between different subject specialisms, and devices are needed to develop interrelations between modules. Examinations can proliferate unless assessment methods are varied. The CNAA requires the student's programme to be 'a balanced education', and so some constraint may be applied to module choice. In general,

> In order to achieve the desired degree of flexibility the Council considers that modules and prerequisites must be very carefully designed, and that this situation will not result from a simple dissection of a number of conventional single-discipline courses . . .

Modular courses, in short, do not write themselves; they need the most careful construction from first principles. But they have been around a long time, and have been developed very satisfactorily up to degree level.

Furthermore, they are now penetrating schools in the shape of CGLI foundation courses, and doing so in direct competition with standard subject-based fare like O-level and CEE. The assertion of *Working Paper 45* that 'teachers . . . think in subject terms' looked sweeping to some of us when it was made in 1972, while we were developing interdisciplinary 11–16 courses in humanities and in creative arts which made use of subjects, but subsumed them beneath an integrating element. But the Schools Council's thinking about the sixth-form curriculum goes back to 1964, and has never convincingly moved much further forward. There is, though, much to admire in *Working Paper 45*, and its underlying argument suggests that given a freer hand, its committee might have reached a quite different solution.

Modular courses and A-level reform

If we sought to rebuild 16–19 education, there can be no doubt that modular courses would be the preferred structure. They offer breadth of choice, effective use of teaching resources, easy transfer to related programmes of study, and the backing of a team of teachers in designing and implementing them. The dangers are well understood: there can be undue fragmentation, too much assessment, too little tutorial control. But that these can be overcome is testified by the success of modular courses in further education, and their popularity with students. Developments like the foundation course at Keele University, modular degree courses in many universities in areas like American studies, and the ten year old success of the Open University confirm that they allow intellectual rigour to be combined with a wider view of the culture. In the tertiary sector, modular courses precisely meet the need we have identified: to link general and directed education, by permitting a course of study to range widely while focusing on some unifying theme of interest. What we should be designing to replace A-level is not another single-subject scenario, but a system of integrated modular courses which would, after all, merely do for A-level students what many of them will find done on degree courses. The fact is that since the Schools Council committees first got their feet under the table, much has happened in non-school areas of education. As Skilbeck (1975) has pointed out, school-based curriculum development may look new to schools, but the principle has been used in higher education for some time. Modular courses would mean such development, but the effort would be worth it both for schools and for the whole nation.

Let us consider how such a system might be organised. It should be possible to devise three levels of modular courses so as to meet the needs of all tertiary students, and much of the work has already been done. At the upper level, we need a set of courses to cope with university entrants, and at the same time profitably engage students with above-average abilities but interests that are somewhat less scholarly. This level would encompass A-level, OND courses and also the BEC and TEC National Diploma courses which will replace OND. Close cooperation with BEC and TEC would therefore be fruitful, since FE and tertiary colleges might ultimately be able to make use of common modules. As a first step, though, the need is to devise a course-based substitute for the three A-level plus general studies course, with a more academic style than OND/BEC/TEC. Let us call it the Advanced National Diploma (AND) course, 'advanced' showing its correspondence to GCE Advanced Level, and 'national' to this level of BEC and TEC courses. Consider, let us say, the AND course in biological sciences. Suppose eight modules are to be completed over the two-year course. Then all AND students, regardless of their subject, might be required to take two *foundation modules*, which would offer units in social studies, philosophy, music and the arts, history of science, consumer and communication skills, politics and economics, and so on. In designing them, use could be made of the IB Theory of Knowledge materials; of recent work on general studies courses; and the short or post-experience courses developed at non-degree level by the Open University. Next, each student would take four *course modules*, and these would correspond roughly to the A-level subject specialisms. The choice for the AND biological sciences course might be just from physics, biology, chemistry and mathematics in a small school sixth form; but a sixth-form or tertiary college would be able to offer a much wider range. Finally, two *option modules* could be chosen from the whole range of subject modules, subject to the guidance of the student's tutor, and *cross-modular assignments* would reinforce the structure.

It might be thought that a broad-ranging programme of this kind would be unacceptable to the average science student. But research suggests quite the reverse. Schools Council *Working Paper 60* (1978) shows that given the chance, most students—whatever their A-level subjects—would prefer a broader curriculum. Thus 95 per cent would choose to study 'at least *one* subject which will significantly develop the skill of numeracy', and 76 per cent would accept the restriction of studying at least one from the arts and social sciences group, and at least one from the mathematics and science group. Also, NFER research by Duckworth (1979) shows that as far as science sixth formers are concerned, 'They achieve better O-level results than non-scientists in most of the subjects they do *not* take in the sixth form'. Contrary to popular belief, the true all-rounders by ability turn out to be science students. But they are ill-served by the present system. Our student with an interest in biological studies would need to take A-levels in biology and chemistry, with physics or mathematics as a third. He would have no opportunity for worthwhile post-O-level studies in English, the arts, social sciences, or in foreign languages. And unless he is luckier than most, his general studies programme will be little more than a haphazard collection of stocking-fillers. The AND course, on the other hand, could offer a broad cultural grounding, plus a choice of science studies, plus courses in French, music, computer studies or whatever at an advanced level.

It might, though, be argued that such a scourse would still not satisfy the demands of university specialist courses. Two counter-points can be made. First, the greater coherence of the AND course, compared with the separate subject basis of N and F and similar proposals, should be an attraction. Second, the decline in tertiary numbers from 1982 onwards will be mirrored in the universities from 1985 onwards. By the end of the 1980s, few universities will be able to afford too diffident an approach to well-researched, closely-argued proposals for a broader sixth-form curriculum.

The AND scheme suggested here is only one of many that might be devised. Some might, for instance, object to it on the grounds that the two compulsory foundation courses impose too rigid a model of breadth: that the breadth of the course does not show enough organic evolution from its focus of interest. An alternative scheme might go for a simpler two-tier module structure, with four course modules and four option modules, but no foundation modules. The biological sciences student might then branch out from his science-based course modules into option units (some perhaps half-rated) in the history and philosophy of science, social studies, political ideas and so on. The basic question is: what rationale are we taking in developing the model that unifies the course around its theme? There seem to be two broad ways of answering this. One is to stick strictly to a rationale arising out of the student's own interest and talents, but informed by the understanding of a wise tutorial counsellor. I see no objection to this, providing the necessary very high degree of student support can be offered. Pragmatic reasoning would incline me towards the alternative, which is to take account of student interests, but develop the broad rationale from some underpinning view of the nature of knowledge. I think, too, that educational reasoning leads to this view. Certainly I would abhor a system which saw breadth in terms of isolated gobbets of knowledge and understanding, and which started and ended with content and on *what* was taught. But in accepting the notion of breadth and balance arising from *how* the course is taught, we still need some map of the culture to help us guide the student, while taking into account his own tastes and preferences. We are leading him to what is surely a mark of the educated adult: to know himself well enough not only to do what comes easily, but also what he may come to do well after initial difficulties. Hence, I think, the case for common-core foundation modules, and it is significant that these are an element of BEC and TEC modular courses and, in even broader terms, of OU degree courses.

Some modules would be independently assessed, while others would be of the Mode-3 type. Continuous assessment and course moderation would be further features, and the two-year AND course could easily be split—as with BEC and TEC schemes—into a one-year certificate course with the second year as a follow-up. Thus a post-16 student might take the first four modules of an AND course as a one-year programme, leaving with an AND certificate to take a job, or perhaps transfer to a similar BEC or TEC national-level course by some agreed system. Flexible arrangements of this kind would be a great improvement on the closed one-year CEE or O-level courses currently under discussion. The AND course at the higher level could be paralleled by the development of Ordinary General Diploma (OGD) courses at the average level of ability, offering parity with O-level and BEC/TEC General courses. Finally, a lower level of course would overlap with CGLI foundation courses and other one-year pre-employment courses. Because of the inherent flexibility of modular schemes, OGD courses could be one or two-year, part or full-time, and cover an ability range stretching, say, from the 30th to the 70th percentile. The flexible way in which many schools have made use of the CSE examination shows that this is perfectly possible, even with a single-subject examination. Course-based approaches offer an extra degree of adaptability.

If courses of this kind were to be introduced, the responsible body would need to represent a variety of interests and command expert advice in planning and implementing the new schemes. Since they would be used in both schools and colleges, an autonomous body with wider interests than the Schools Council would seem to be indicated, and the new coordinating body postulated by the Labour administration in 1979 to administer the GCSE is a precedent for this. The experience of TEC and BEC would be valuable, but the curriculum design of the new courses should be from first principles. A particular need is to get away from the preoccupation with behavioural aims-objectives models which has marred much of the TEC work so far, and BEC courses to a lesser extent. No doubt it is a temptation in designing modules to seek detailed statements of learning objectives, but behavioural means-ends models have little to commend them, beyond the transfer of information and training in simple skills. 'Knowledge is primarily concerned with synthesis. The analytic approach implied in the objectives model readily trivialises it' (Stenhouse 1975). Our concern must also be with the process of teaching, and teachers and lecturers need scope to develop their own strategies for implementing general aims. Means and ends can be interactive, and Hirst (1973) has suggested ways in which we can identify curriculum outcomes without a commitment to behavioural objectives. There is no reason why the development of curriculum modules should not proceed on lines which give the very greatest autonomy to teachers and the course team, making use of a rationale of curriculum which sees curriculum process and product as a unity.

The kind of scheme that has been proposed here would need the authority of a commission of inquiry behind it if it were to be implemented. But I have argued in Chapter 1 that the problems of tertiary education are too extensive, too expensive and involve too many overlapping interests to allow merely piecemeal solutions. Consider, for example, the costly interventions of the MSC into 16-plus training programmes; without any coordinating machinery, we have the spectacle of some students being paid to do what others must learn at their own expense. There is no reason why the middle and lower levels of modular courses outlined above should not be tied in with the sort of courses run by TOPS and with other MSC initiatives: there is built-in scope for alternating college modules with work experience in any modular scheme. But to make a new synthesis in the tertiary sector requires an authoritative voice.

The emphasis must assuredly be on synthesis rather than compromise, which has proved an unreliable lodestar for the Schools Council. In response to criticism of the N and F scheme as a compromise, the joint chairmen of its Joint Examinations Sub-Committee wrote to the *The Times Educational Supplement* (12.5.78) to say:

> We regard this response as evidence for the good sense and democratic working of the council . . . All the evidence possessed by the council suggests that . . . there is a good chance of something like the N and F scheme's being generally accepted. If this is compromise, please can we have more of it?

But it is the kind of compromise which aims to please everybody, and ends up pleasing nobody. The final fate of the N and F scheme proved to be very different from that envisaged for it by the Schools Council. Compromise makes a poor rallying call: the trumpet has an uncertain sound.

But the problems of tertiary education cannot be solved by a single Utopian stroke, and an evolutionary timetable will be needed, making full use of the BEC and TEC developments and of CGLI foundation courses. Modular courses cannot be introduced in place of O and A-level overnight; the greatest care will be needed in harmonising with other interests in the field, quite apart from problems of curriculum design and in-service education for teachers. New support initiatives will be needed to link schools and colleges with the coordinating body. But once a national commission has made a fresh synthesis and given a clear lead, the necessary means can be willed.

Some immediate problems

All this will take time, and we still await the setting up of a national inquiry as a first step. In the meantime, a number of issues clamour for attention.

First, there is the need to introduce greater breadth into the three A-level programme and somehow widen the scope of A-level to reach more students. In my view the four F-level proposal was the best interim solution, since it would have been relatively easy to prune enough dead wood from an existing A-level to make it three-quarters as extensive, and yet just as demanding of the intellect. And F-level was close enough to the gold standard of A-level to make it an acceptable political move. It would then have been a straightforward matter to require each university entrant to take one arts subject (including languages) and one maths or science subject. Given an early decision, the 4F scheme could have been operating by 1986. But the 1979 Thatcher administration has opted for the unqualified retention of A-level. If nothing is done to re-open a discussion of alternatives to this unsatisfactory examination, we are likely to see more colleges establishing the International Baccalaureate for their ablest students. This would help to focus attention on the virtues of broad whole-curriculum courses. But the IB can do little of direct value for a wider range of ability, and augmenting A-level with CEE or AO subjects would not deal with the real issues. If our membership of the EEC is to count for much in terms of post-16 educational links, we must think hard about our commitment to a tertiary system totally at variance with the pattern preferred by our European partners.

The second problem is that of resources, institutions and falling rolls. It is one problem because these are interactive aspects. Falling rolls will lead to fewer school sixth forms and more 16–19 institutions; to fewer resources in schools for minority courses; and as schools feel the pinch, students who can will move to colleges where choice flourishes. And if falling rolls make tertiary colleges more attractive than sixth-form colleges, there is even less reason to bother with new courses under school regulations when such a variety of courses already exists in tertiary colleges operating under FE regulations. Any blurring of the distinction between the two sets of regulations would facilitate the transplant of FE courses into sixth-form colleges and larger school sixth forms. The general trend here is clear enough. Small 16–19 units are costly to run, and can do the education of their students a disservice. And larger units, whether self contained or federally linked, will tend to introduce sooner or later an FE element. Even if the union remains unblessed, the school and FE sectors are moving ever closer.

This, then, is a problem which will be solved by economic pressures, but it is important that local solutions keep educational issues in mind, and DES support for the tertiary-college solution should be backed up by a greater willingness to consider the problems of 16–19 education as a whole. And the economic solution also puts in perspective the problem of CEE and one-year courses; for the problem goes away, once school and sixth-form students can gain access to the BEC/TEC general and CGLI vocational courses through

FE or tertiary colleges. By the time the Keohane Committee's CEE scheme has been duly ratified, it will look very much like a stop-gap measure to meet the short-term needs of schools and sixth-form colleges. For in the longer run, the logical answer of course-based FE-type solutions will have been forced on them by purely financial considerations.

In practice, things will not work out so tidily as this, and much painful agonising will be gone through. But I think one can argue that even without some overt attempt to rationalise the school-college scene, we can see that cost pressures will take us at least some part of the way. And in curriculum terms, that means CEE is purely an expedient, to tide us over the transition period; an examination we could do without if the transition were speeded up.

This is an advantage, because it means the decks are clear to tackle the third problem: of encouraging schools to use their subject specialisms in more enterprising ways, and in particular to look at modular, interest-focused courses for tertiary students. We can expect CGLI foundation courses to become more popular, and to challenge the CEE over the lower half of the ability range. This will be helpful. But the difficulties of A-level courses can only be solved by a flexible, modular solution which allows not only a wider engagement with two-year students, but a new range of one-year courses which can be either self-contained, or contributory to the two-year course. Furthermore, modular courses make this possible with economic use of resources, and so offer medium-sized school sixth forms the best hope of survival. Two-tier single-subject schemes like N + F, or N + A, fail on all these counts. They have no curriculum potential, and money spent in developing them is money wasted.

It might be argued that schools are so wedded to a subject-focused approach to the curriculum that, despite the advent of CGLI foundation courses, adopting a modular structure would be too much of an upheaval. But it is worth noting that the introduction of BEC General to replace, for example, COS courses in further education has been by no means a painless affair. Although the COS course involves a broad field of study (Chapter 2), the separate subject lecturers would rarely come together for conjoint planning of the course. BEC General requires exactly this kind of cooperation in seeking a unified treatment of its integrating themes, and the experience of getting together as a team round a table has been a novel one in many colleges. And in business studies lecturers may often be part-time, with contributory skills quite narrowly defined. The key roles of the BEC moderator in sorting out assessment problems, and of the college coordinator in bringing the team of staff together to plan the course, should not be underestimated. There seems no fundamental reason why a similar operation could not be carried out in the context of a school.

We are left with the fourth, and final, problem: that of linking these solutions to post-16 unemployment and nagging questions about manpower planning and the competing claims of continuous and continuing education. These are matters for Government-level debate rather than local improvisations. But they will arise with any far-reaching reforms, and there seems little point in financing any other kind of reform. In establishing the TEC courses, for example, the Technician Education Council has needed to link with the City and Guilds Foundation, where it is taking over its technician-level work; with the joint councils responsible for running the higher and national diploma and certificate engineering courses; and with the Manpower Services Commission in trying to secure credit transfer between TEC courses and MSC courses like those of the Training Opportunities Scheme. Negotiation of this kind would be a great deal easier if major departments of state like the DES made it their business to frame policies. This, it would seem, is what Governments are for. Without a policy, we can hope only to muddle through at a time when increasing international competition makes it more necessary than ever to develop tertiary education along the most effective lines.

The arguments put forward in this book are not, in themselves, new. But in setting the problems of the school sixth form against the wider background of other forms of tertiary education and training, my hope must be that the arguments look more compelling, and capable of generating some useful solutions. Most of the discussion about the sixth form since the Crowther Report has failed to put it in the perspective of developments outside the school sector, and has concentrated on its examinations rather than its curriculum. Although the professed intention has usually been to put curriculum first, the lack of any genuinely developmental approach has led inevitably to solutions in which examination structures emerge as a poor substitute for curriculum thinking. And an unswerving commitment to single-subject examinations has given the *coup de grace* to any fresh initiative.

Two notable exceptions are first, the admirable work done by Peterson (1973), which has come to fruition in the International Baccalaureate; and second, the Dainton Report of 1968, which, despite the rather instrumental concern of its terms of reference with the supply of scientists and technologists to fuel the economy, shows a much more enlightened view of the sixth-form curriculum than many other documents with loftier intentions. One quotation must suffice:

> There is an urgent need more rapidly to infuse breadth, humanity and up-to-dateness into the science curriculum and its teaching . . . Specialisation there must be to get to the frontiers of knowledge and to stimulate and expand intellectual powers and critical abilities; and in some limited sense it should probably begin in the sixth form. But it is all the more effective—and indeed

attractive—for being set upon a broad base of intellectual achievement. It is not synonymous with a formal code of massive factual content; nor . . . need it be incompatible with a breadth of study offering intellectual rigour and challenge.

This seems to me a shrewd analysis of what is wrong with so much sixth-form work, and a valuable pointer in a fresh and rewarding direction. And it is perhaps no coincidence that the Dainton Committee's membership extended beyond the limits of school experience which have cramped the Schools Council's deliberations on the same kinds of issues. What is regrettable is that all this was said, but unheard, so long ago.

In some respects, the decision in June 1979 of the Conservative Secretary of State to allow A-level to continue unchanged must be greeted with mixed feelings. Although the N and F proposals were always an unsatisfactory compromise, the 4F scheme did at least represent some yielding of ground by the universities in the cause of greater breadth. But now that N and F have been shelved, the way is open for the critics of A-level to urge a fresh look at the whole problem, and one which takes account—as the Schools Council never has—of the entire 16–19 context and the educational demands which the world of 2001 will make on our citizens. No one in their senses can possibly pretend that A-level is the ideal examination for today, let alone tomorrow. The trouble is that all of the proposed cures have been worse than the disease.

Any administration seriously concerned to see 16–19 education as a means of strengthening our economic competitiveness and enriching our lives must tackle the fundamental issues at national level. The decision to reject N and F should therefore be taken not as a vote for A-level in the sixth forms of the twenty-first century, but a vote against the wrong kind of A-level substitute. And if a better solution is to be found in time to improve our international chances, there is no time to lose. A new scheme for the mid-eighties could also take account of falling rolls in the tertiary sector, and turn this to advantage. As the 11–16 school moves hesitantly towards a common school-based curriculum, account must be taken of the rise and rise of the sixth form college, and the emergence—as one would expect, by chance rather than design—of the tertiary college. Examination planning in the tertiary sector must start with curriculum planning, and seize the opportunity to develop new, unified concepts around these new institutions.

APPENDIX A
A Federal Solution: the Cambridge Collegiate Board

The following brief account of the development and operation of the Cambridge Collegiate Board has been prepared by its Secretary, Peter Bryan.

The Collegiate Board came into existence in June 1973, one year ahead of the beginning of comprehensive education in the Cambridge area in September 1974. This enabled the board to spend a year planning the detailed operation of the provisions of the reorganisation plan agreed between the local education authority and the Department of Education and Science, particularly the rationalisation of courses and the institution of a common system of application for all full-time courses in the six centres. The concept of the Collegiate Board is an integral part of the reorganisation plan, not an *ad hoc* organisation, and its inclusion was one of the main reasons for DES approval of that part of the plan which dealt with 16–19 education.

The board's operations cover an area of some fifteen to twenty miles around Cambridge, an area which looks to the city as its natural regional centre. The scheme embraces some fifteen main feeder schools, which are 11–16 units, but altogether students are drawn from about twenty-five units, since there is a significant inflow from private as well as maintained schools.

All pupils transfer at 16, apart from a very few exceptional cases. This means that the six Collegiate Board centres are drawing from a year group of about two and a half thousand pupils, nearly two-thirds of whom apply to stay on full time. Allowing for subsequent withdrawals after initial application, this means that some 45 per cent of the year group are eventually enrolled.

The six Collegiate Board centres are:

(a) two colleges of further education—
   (i) the Cambridgeshire College of Arts and Technology which offers a wide range of A-level, TEC and BEC courses;
   (ii) the Cambridge College of Further Education which at present offers a wide variety of vocational courses and O-level courses with a vocational bias;

(b) two sixth-form colleges—Hills Road Sixth Form College and Long Road Sixth Form College—which offer GCE courses at A, AO, and O-level;

(c) two sixth forms in 11–18 schools—Impington Village College and Netherhall School—which are the only exceptions to the local basic form of organisation into 11–16 schools. They offer A-level courses only.

The Collegiate Board itself consists of the principals of these six centres. The Secretary to the Collegiate Board is a full-time officer whose sole duties are the work of the board. He is appointed as a headmaster under Burnham Regulations, and is on the staff of the Chief Education Officer. His main responsibilities are:

(a) to operate the entry scheme to the six centres, which is designed on UCCA principles;

(b) to monitor and develop the whole field of 16–19 education, acting as a link between the board, the Chief Education Officer and his staff, the careers service, the 11–16 feeder schools, parents and pupils;

(c) to conduct research into educational matters affecting the board's operations, to collate information needed by the board to formulate policy decisions, and to prepare the necessary documents for the board and Education Committee.

The board meets about twice a term, and on these occasions at least one education officer, a senior careers officer and an 11–16 school headmaster are present, together with any other persons invited because of their expert knowledge of a topic under discussion. In its discussions, the board is dealing with two main areas:

(a) It is enjoined by the Education Committee to monitor, guide and develop 16–19 education as a whole, embracing both the school and further education sectors. The members of the board are therefore obliged not only to represent their own centres, but also to act collectively in making policy for the area as a whole. Major policy decisions must however be endorsed by the Education Committee. A significant aspect of this function is to see that the resources available are used as efficiently as possible, and to this end, the board agrees collectively on the courses which will be run by each centre. The principals discuss their course structure annually, and agree not to make unilateral decisions on their provision. In this way unnecessary duplication is avoided, which leads to considerable efficiency in operation, and the resources which are thereby released are devoted to widening the range of opportunities available. The executive powers which the board possesses mean that decisions in these fields carry the authority of the Education Committee and cannot be set aside other than with the board's agreement.

(b) The board is responsible for operating an entry scheme to all courses in the school and further education colleges. A single application form enables pupils to apply for all courses in all centres. They will have gained details of the courses from a wide variety of sources, including a booklet which every pupil receives at sixteen. The board sees it as a major responsibility that students and parents should have placed before them details and advice on all post-sixteen opportunities in education, full and part-time, in schools and further education; and that students should be free to select the course they wish without pressure from any quarter. This implies an elaborate system of talks, interviews, and open evenings, which is constantly developing in cooperation with 11–16 feeder schools.

By instituting the Collegiate Board, the authority hopes to have steered a middle course between the wasteful competition and duplication which attend complete independence, and an undesirably rigid control which would inhibit initiative. It recognises the need for planning and requires from the board firm recommendations for consideration by the authority, but it does not take from the members their professional authority in making educational decisions.

APPENDIX B
Exeter College: a summary of tertiary college organisation

The first tertiary college was opened in Exeter in 1970, by closing the sixth forms in the Exeter local authority schools and concentrating all post-16 provision at the city's technical college, renamed Exeter College. Its principal since 1970, Philip Merfield, has provided the following outline of its structure and the courses offered (for a general view of tertiary colleges and their arrangements, see Janes and Miles 1978).

The college is a large enterprise: in 1978 there were 1650 full-time students, along with 3000 part-time day students and 2500 attending classes in the evening. Its 16–19 students come chiefly from the six 12–16 comprehensive schools in Exeter, but there are close links with another six schools outside the city, information links with another ten or so, and link courses with eight schools. The six Exeter schools have a particularly close relationship with the college; they are represented on the Exeter Academic Council, and there is a joint liaison committee of representatives from the schools and the college. There are some exchanges of teachers, and a number of joint curriculum working parties. The college has an agreed catchment area in relation to neighbouring colleges of further education. There is a centrally administered admissions system.

In addition to a governing body, there is an academic board with six committees, responsible for: executive matters (the principal, the two vice-principals, and the seven heads of department); admissions and advisory services; course development; inter-departmental matters; resources for learning; and staff development.

The academic work is arranged under seven departments: business studies; arts and humanities; building and civil engineering; engineering (these latter two combining for administrative and resource purposes as the faculty of technology); food and fashion; social studies; and science and mathematics.

The pastoral system has two elements. First, every student, whether full or part-time, has a *course tutor*. Students taking GCE subject examinations choose a key subject, the teacher of which becomes their tutor with an extra time allowance. Second, there are a number of *specialist advisers*, to whom students and staff have easy access: a counsellor; a careers and admissions officer; a senior resources tutor; a tutor for overseas students and higher education; an Oxbridge tutor; a college nurse; and a staff development officer.

Formal links with industry exist through eight advisory committees. But there are close links, too, with the industrial training boards; the Training Services Agency; and through many short training courses for industry. Many staff are engaged in the committees of professional bodies, and in the development of TEC and BEC courses. Almost all have graduate, professional or technical qualifications. Examination successes are up to or above the national average in both GCE and vocational courses.

The college has special strengths in several types of work. It acts as the East Devon Area College for a wide range of courses up to HNC or advanced craft and technician levels, with notable courses in public administration and civil engineering. On the GCE side, the college has developed special courses focused on physical education, art, music and drama. These have led to strong cultural activities in drama, orchestra, choral society and various sports clubs. The college sports teams have proved outstandingly successful in county and regional competitions.

A-level courses are offered in 35 subjects: accounts, art, biology, botany, chemistry, computer science, economics, engineering drawing, engineering science, English, French, geography, geology, German, geometrical drawing (building), government and politics, history, history of art, home economics, Latin, law, mathematics (applied), mathematics (pure), mathematics (pure with computations), music, physics, physics (with electronics), religious knowledge, Russian, sociology, statistics, surveying, textiles and dress, woodwork, and zoology. Many subjects are available on a one-year as well as a two-year basis, and part-time including evenings.

O-level courses are offered in the usual school subjects, together with: accounts, British constitution, building construction, commerce, drama and theatre arts, economic and social history, economics, engineering science, environmental studies, food and nutrition, geology, geometrical drawing (building), Greek literature in translation, human biology, law, Russian, Spanish, social economics, sociology, statistics, surveying, textiles and dress. There are classes for those repeating subjects, and part-time, including evening, courses.

CEE courses are not offered. The needs of one-year students are met either by O-level courses, or by the vocational courses summarised in the next paragraph, or by foundation courses (see below).

Other courses include OND courses in building, business studies, hotel and catering operations, and technology (engineering); there are 'special interest' courses in drama and physical education. Other courses, which may be for one or two years and which usually lead to City and Guilds certificates, RSA or London Chamber of Commerce examinations, are held in: secretarial and office work; electrical, mechanical and motor vehicle engineering; building; catering; reception work; hairdressing; nursing; child and community care. Most of these are available part-time too. The new range of technician-level courses for the awards of the Business and Technician Education Councils are being rapidly developed.

Non-examination courses, as general studies, are part of the programme of all full-time GCE students: they consist of courses in recreational activities and personal education, and are organised through the pastoral system. The tutors in identified 'key' subjects have extra time in which to go beyond the examination syllabus and make connections with other subjects and with life in general. There are about 15 students in each pastoral group.

This extensive range of courses is characteristic of all tertiary colleges. Exeter's list of nearly forty GCE courses reflects its large number of full-time students: at 1650, this is three times larger than the total at many tertiary colleges. All the tertiary colleges offer considerable economies of scale: Exeter's range of courses is possible on a staff:student ratio of 1:12.5. In 1977/78, the net cost per full-time equivalent student was approximately £725 per annum. It should be noted, too, that over and above normal tuition fees, the college has been able to generate about £150,000 in fee income per annum by the development of Industrial Training Board and other 'self-supporting' courses.

The size of Exeter College brings advantages: but the staff are well aware of the danger that students or staff might feel lost or anonymous. We believe we have preserved human scale and the chance of individual recognition by a judicious combination of college democracy; departmental management and reference point; and tutorial base, with good support from specialist services and counsellors.

The novelty of the whole institution encourages a spirit of experiment, and the college has investigated many new ways of running courses, organising its internal management structure and liaising with local schools. This should make it better able to cope with the rapid changes that result from external circumstance, e.g. restrictions on finance, cooperation with external agencies (industrial training boards, the Training Services Agency, the Manpower Services Commission, BEC, TEC and so on), and new local authority controls or procedures. Complacency and a quiet life are impossible in a tertiary college, and probably inappropriate today in any educational institution.

Examples of such innovation might include:

(a) *Key subject courses*—where GCE A-level work is given a coherent course structure as a base for tutorial control, corporate spirit and general studies. It is possible, too, to combine A-level with vocational courses.

(b) *Foundation courses*—for students who are not wholly academic nor vocational in their interests or aptitudes. These combine O-levels with vocational subjects or with special interest elements such as PE, drama, commercial subjects and child care.

(c) *Staff participation*—via a powerful academic board and committee structure incorporating the Management Group as an Executive Committee.

(d) *School links*—via a liaison committee with feeder schools as part of an umbrella structure for the whole Exeter educational system.

Glossary of Terms

Advanced Level (A-Level) *see* General Certificate of Education

Assessment of Performance Unit. A unit within the Department of Education and Science (q.v.), set up in 1974 'to promote the development of methods of assessing and monitoring the achievement of children at school, and to seek to identify the incidents of under-achievement'. Subsequently, the emphasis has shifted from under-achievement to the monitoring of educational standards. Random samples of children aged 11, 13 and 15 will be tested on a number of kinds of development. The first results, in mathematics, are due for publication in 1979. Language and science will follow. Monitoring in personal and social development, aesthetic development and physical development is still under discussion.

Business Education Council (BEC). An independent body set up in 1974 to provide 'a national system of non-degree courses . . . within the broad area of business and public administration'. Its courses have a modular construction (*see* Modular Courses) and are offered at three levels: at each level a certificate or diploma is available. *BEC General* courses, at the first level, correspond to the level of the Certificate in Office Studies (q.v.) A certificate can be awarded after one year's part-time study: a diploma after one year full-time, or two years part-time. *BEC National* courses are equivalent to the level of the Ordinary National Diploma (q.v.) in Business Studies. They qualify for entry of Dip HE (q.v.) and degree courses, and are thus on a par with a course made up of 2 or 3 A-levels (q.v.). *BEC Higher National* courses are technical awards at degree level.

Certificate of Extended Education (CEE). An extended form of the Certificate of Secondary Education (CSE; q.v.) first proposed by the Schools Council (q.v.) in 1970, and intended for one-year students in school sixth forms (q.v.). It is a single-subject examination for students with entry grades 2-4 in CSE, and students are expected to take a course made up of 4 or 5 such subjects. Trial schemes exist, and it is used in some schools and many sixth-form colleges (q.v.). In 1979 the Keohane Committee recommended national approval of a modified CEE.

Certificate of Further Education (CFE). A one-year post-16 course under development in further education (q.v.) institutions, intended for students with entry qualifications at an average level of CSE grades 2-4; possibly slightly above the level of City and Guilds foundation courses (q.v.) but slightly below that of the Certificate in Office Studies (q.v.). It differs from the Certificate of Extended Education (q.v.) in that it has a vocational commitment, and is awarded for a whole course of study, rather than for study of a single subject forming only part of a course. It has been slow to catch on, and its general value is as yet uncertain.

Certificate of Office Studies (COS). An important further-education course introduced in 1963 as a part-time two-year programme of study for young office workers. In 1971 one-year full and part-time variants were introduced. It is in course of replacement by BEC General certificate and diploma courses (q.v.). It is examined by the National Committee for the COS and can lead to ONC and OND courses (q.v.) in business studies, or BEC National courses.

Certificate of Secondary Education (CSE). An examination introduced in 1965 for 16-plus pupils. Like GCE O-level (q.v.), which it complements, it is a single subject examination. In a given subject, O-level is designed to cater for the top 20 per cent of the ability range, and CSE for the next 40 per cent. There is no public 16-plus examination designed for the bottom 40 per cent. Five grades are awarded, and grade 4 indicates average ability. Grade 1 is equivalent to an O-level pass at an unstated grade. The CSE is intended to test the results of a five-year course and may be examined in Modes 1, 2 or 3 (q.v.). It is proposed to subsume the CSE within the common GCSE examination (q.v.).

City and Guilds of London Institute (CGLI). An independent body founded in 1878 by the Corporation and livery companies of the City of London for the furtherance of technical education. It has offered since 1879 a wide range of examinations at operative, craftsman, technician and technologist level.

City and Guilds Foundation Courses were first introduced as pilot schemes in schools and colleges in 1975. A CGLI foundation course is 'a programme of full-time education designed to development the interests, abilities and talents of young people, to satisfy their vocational needs and to provide a basis for integrating and continuing their general education'. They are for students of about average ability, and are generally taken on a one or two-year basis, starting in the sixth form (or first year in a further-education college) or possibly in the fifth form of a school. Each course is based on a broad occupational theme, like engineering or distribution, and has a modular basis (q.v.). Schools and colleges may design their own foundation courses, and students on the courses may also be preparing for other examinations like CSE and O-level (q.v.). Assessment is undertaken jointly by the CGLI and teachers. The courses are emerging as an increasingly popular alternative in schools to courses based on a number of CEE subjects.

College of Higher Education. An institution offering courses up to degree level, and often based on a former college of education. Its courses may have a broad vocational commitment, often after a Dip HE (q.v.) course has been taken within the college.

Council for National Academic Awards (CNAA). An autonomous body established by Royal Charter in 1964 to award degrees to students in education institutions, such as colleges of higher education and polytechnics (q.v.). Thus the binary system of higher education, with CNAA degrees and university degrees, reflects at this level the division between school and college, and between academic and technical education.

County Colleges. These were recommended in the 1944 Education Act for the provision of compulsory further education post-16 for students not otherwise receiving formal education. They have never been implemented.

Crowther Report. A report of the Central Advisory Council for Education (England) under the chairmanship of Sir Geoffrey Crowther, published in 1959 under the title *15-18*. Its espousal of the principle of 'study in depth' in the sixth form has been under attack since its publication. The report did, however, argue strongly for county colleges (q.v.).

Department of Education and Science (DES). The department of national government which replaced the Ministry of Education in 1963, and responsible for policy in education and scientific research. Its head is the Secretary of State, and it is responsible for schools, further education (q.v.) and higher education (q.v.). Its officials are permanent civil servants. It is responsible for ensuring that its policies are implemented by local education authorities (q.v.).

Diploma in Higher Education (Dip HE). A post-18 but pre-degree qualification proposed by the James Committee on teacher education and training in 1972. In its emphasis on the need to combine study in depth with a broadly based education, the proposals had some similarity with the International Baccalaureate (q.v.). Dip HE courses have not proved particularly popular, but the two-year Dip HE can serve both as a terminal qualification and as the first part of an honours degree. It would become attractive if the four-year honours degree course became a reality, and follow on well from an integrated tertiary course in school or college.

Diploma in Technology (Dip Tech). A national award of honours degree standard particularly for students taking advanced sandwich courses. Although now replaced by CNAA bachelors' degrees, its establishment in 1958 marked the first award of degree standard to be granted by a non-university body.

Further Education (FE). Full-time post-16 education is available either in schools, or in colleges operating under FE regulations. These include technical colleges, tertiary colleges (q.v.) and colleges of further education. FE colleges are administered, like schools, by local education authorities (q.v.), but the regulations are different. Only colleges, for example, may take part-time students. Although GCE A-level courses (q.v.) are offered in both schools and colleges, the main business of the colleges is with vocational courses. But the line between vocational and academic courses is increasingly difficult to draw. (q.v. Higher Education).

General Certificate of Education (GCE). An examination first introduced in 1951 at three levels: Ordinary (O-level) at 15 or 16-plus; Advanced (A-level) as a terminal 18-plus examination; and Scholarship (S-level) for those going on to university. It was a single-subject examination, with no grouping, and students were not required to take the examinations successively at the three levels. In practice, O-level is taken at 16-plus, since five subjects at O-level are generally a minimum requirement for higher education; and S-level has been absorbed into A-level, in the form of additional 'special' papers which are rarely taken.

General Certificate of Secondary Education (GCSE). A common system of 16-plus examination recommended by the 1978 White Paper, for introduction by the mid-1980s. The plan has been shelved by the 1979 Conservative administration. The divided system of GCE O-level (q.v.) for the top 20 per cent of the ability range, and CSE (q.v.) for the next 40 per cent, would be replaced by a single system under 4 or 5 examining authorities to cover England and Wales. GCSE would be a single-subject examination, like GCE and CSE, with certificates awarded on a single seven-point grading scale: the top three points would be equivalent to the present O-level grades A, B and C, and the other four to the CSE grades 2-5.

General Studies. A programme of studies designed to complement the more specialised character of A-level courses in schools and colleges, and usually offered to one-year sixth-formers as well. They are mainly not examined, but general studies examinations exist at O-level, AO (alternative O)-level, and at A-level. They may take up from 5 to 30 per cent of total time. The *General Studies Association* exists to promote them as a broadening influence on the curriculum.

Grammar School. A selective secondary school maintained by a local education authority and admitting the top 15 to 30 per cent of the 11-plus age group by means of ability or achievement tests. Such schools tend to have large sixth forms catering mainly for entrants to higher education.

Her Majesty's Inspectorate. A body of inspectors (HMIs) attached to the DES (q.v.) but separately responsible to the Secretary of State. Their role was defined in 1840 as one of assistance rather than control, and was muted during the 1960s. Since the mid-seventies their opinions have been more in evidence.

Higher Education. Study at the level of a degree or above, carried out in a university, polytechnic or college or higher education as a rule. The term may also be used to describe work beyond A-level standard (or its equivalent), for example at a college of education. A distinction sometimes made is between non-advanced further education (post-16, and up to A-level) and advanced further education (post A-level). The former may be termed tertiary education, the latter shades into higher education (q.v.).

Higher School Certificate (HSC). A post-16 examination replaced by GCE A-level in 1951. Unlike A-level, it was a two-tier examination at principal and subsidiary level, and for most of its life principal subjects were chosen from prescribed groups.

International Baccalaureate (IB). A complete programme of post-16 study for entrants to international higher-education institutions, first available in 1967. Subjects are offered at higher and subsidiary level in a grouped pattern to ensure breadth of study. A course in the theory of knowledge is compulsory, with the aim of promoting coherence.

Liberal Studies. Essentially a synonym for general studies (q.v.) commonly used in FE colleges rather than schools. The 1956 proposals for the Dip Tech (q.v.) insisted that liberal studies were to be included, and these courses became a feature of further education in the sixties as an offset to the vocational emphasis of some programmes. But with the growing development of courses incorporating broader study, and some uncertainty about the exact purpose of these courses, there are signs of a shift towards an integrated approach to breadth of study. Like sixth-form general studies, they suffer from their disconnection with the main body of examined work.

Local Education Authority. The responsible local body for the administration of education in schools and colleges. It may cover a large rural or a small urban area. Its policy is determined, subject to limits set by the DES (q.v.), by a committee of the locally elected council and carried out by permanent officials under a chief education officer, and usually including a team of advisers (sometimes termed inspectors) with responsibility for particular levels or subjects.

Manpower Services Commission. A quasi-autonomous body set up under the Department of Employment in 1974 with responsibility for publicly provided post-16 training. It includes representatives of employers, trade unions, local authorities and education. Its training provision is the responsibility of the Training Services Division. It provides training and work experience for 16–19 year olds under the Training for Skills programme, including the Training Opportunities Scheme (TOPS), and for unemployed young people under the Youth Opportunities Programme. Its provisions overlap, and to some extent compete with, those offered by schools and further education since students on MSC courses receive training grants.

Modes 1, 2, 3. Terms to describe modes of examining first introduced by the CSE boards (q.v.). Mode 1 examinations are set and marked by a board using the board's own syllabus; Mode 2 are set by the school and marked by the board; Mode 3 set and marked by the school. Very little Mode 2 examining is done, and the take-up of Mode 3 has been generally disappointing. The option of Mode 3 would be retained under the proposals for the GCSE examination (q.v.).

Modern School. Under post-war reorganisation, secondary modern schools were to provide 'a good all-round education . . . developing out of the interests of the children' for those not selected for traditional grammar-school education (q.v.). The modern schools thus continued the traditions of the elementary schools, and in most cases were the same schools with the name changed. They were to have 'parity of esteem' with the grammar schools, but have given way to comprehensive schools. In a few areas technical high schools (q.v.) were also built.

Modular Course. Four distinguishing features of a modular course are: (i) it will be largely constructed from options under the control of the student; (ii) the optioned sections form self-contained modules; (iii) assessment is mainly linked to performance on individual modules, rather than to the whole course; (iv) final grading is based on accumulated module credits. Such courses can combine a broad programme of study with a unifying focus of interest for the course as a whole.

N and F Scheme. A proposal, first launched in Schools Council *Working Paper 45* (1972), for the replacement of A-level by a two-tier programme. Instead of the usual A-level course, a student would take five subjects to N-level (rated at half an A-level each) over two years, with the possibility of further study in up to two subjects to F-level (rated at three-quarters of an A-level). Thus 3N + 2F would have an equivalent rating to three A-levels. General studies would be retained. The five subjects would, it was hoped, be chosen to cover a broad field of study. The proposals were rejected by the 1979 Conservative Secretary for Education (Mr Carlisle).

Open University (OU). A university established in 1969 by royal charter to enable any resident of the United Kingdom over 21 to obtain a degree by study at home rather than by residence at an institution. Its study texts and materials are supplemented by radio and TV programmes, and backed up by a tutorial service and, for some courses, a residential summer school. In 1979 75,000 people were studying with the OU, and a further 27,000 had obtained degrees.

Ordinary Level (O-level)   *see* General Certificate of Education.

Ordinary National Diploma (OND). A course available only under further education regulations (q.v.) for post-16 students, roughly comparable in standard to GCE A-level (q.v.) A two-year full-time course might include a sandwich element of industrial study, leading to an OND in agriculture, business studies, engineering etc. A part-time course offers less depth of coverage and leads to an Ordinary National Certificate (ONC). Unlike A-level, the course is assessed as a complete programme rather than in terms of separate subjects. The OND and ONC courses will eventually be replaced by BEC and TEC national courses (q.v.)

Organisation for Economic Cooperation and Development (OECD). A body set up in 1960 to promote economic growth and world trade. Its member countries are Australia, Austria,

Belgium, Canada, Denmark, Finland, France, West Germany, Greece, Iceland, Ireland, Italy, Japan, Luxembourg, the Netherlands, New Zealand, Norway, Portugal, Spain, Sweden, Switzerland, Turkey, the United Kingdom and the United States.

Polytechnics. Most students taking CNAA (q.v.) degree courses are in the 30 polytechnics in England and Wales, which were set up after the 1966 White Paper. They also provide sub-degree and post-graduate courses, short courses, and take both full and part-time students. Their courses generally have a vocational slant, but there has been growth in arts and social sciences courses as well as in science and technology courses.

Post-compulsory Education. Term used to describe any course of study designed for students beyond the school leaving age of 16, but often associated with sub-degree work and 16–19 education in particular.

Public School. In Britain, a term generally applied to those private, independent schools whose head teachers are in membership of the Headmasters' Conference, first established in 1869, and amounting to about 250 schools. The entry age is usually 13, and most pupils will stay into the sixth form. The ethos of most HMC schools owes much to their Victorian origins, and pupils are predominantly boarders and single sex, although coeducation in the sixth form is increasing. The size of public school sixth forms gives them an influence on university entrance in greater proportion than the total size of the sector would suggest. Thus *DES Statistics* (Vol 1, 1976) show that 18 per cent of 16–19 students in 1976 were in fee-paying schools (i.e. all independent schools, not merely the HMC schools), although the proportion of fee-paying pupils in all secondary education is only 8 per cent.

Royal Society of Arts (RSA). An independent body granted a royal charter in 1847 for the advancement of science in connexion with arts, manufactures and commerce. It conducts a wide range of examinations, particularly in commercial subjects and modern languages, which may be used both in schools and FE institutions.

Schools Council. A body set up in 1964 with responsibility for curriculum development in schools, and for GCE and CSE examinations (q.v.) through the area examining boards. It is financed jointly by the DES (q.v.) and local education authorities (q.v.). Its constitution was last revised in 1978, but the influence of teachers' organisations is still controlling on most of its committees. Since 1964 it has been committed to the reform of the sixth-form curriculum, culminating in the N and F proposals (q.v.).

Secondary Education. Education over the 11–18 range in schools is generally termed secondary education. Since comprehensive reorganisation some intermediate schools have been formed, overlapping primary (5–11) and secondary (11–18) education. These are termed middle schools.

Sixth Form. A term believed to have originated at Winchester College, a public school (q.v.) in the seventeenth century, when the sixth form became the highest in the school. In the 11–16 school the sixth year is the first post-16 year, and the second for two-year students will be the seventh. But in general these will be called the lower and upper sixth, in deference to the tradition that the sixth form offers a form of education distinctive from that in the main 11–16 school.

Standing Conference on University Entrance (SCUE). A body established in 1965 on the initiative of the Committee of Vice-Chancellors and Principals (CVCP). It has a permanent secretary; a chairman nominated by the CVCP; 8 members who also serve on the Schools Council; 4 members nominated by the Scottish Universities Council on Entrance; and members nominated by individual universities in England, Wales and Northern Ireland, giving a total membership of over 60. Its brief is to discuss the implications for universities of developments in school curricula and examinations, coordinate university policy on entrance, and serve as a link between the universities and the Schools Council. SCUE is therefore an influential body in any matters concerning the sixth-form curriculum and the reform of A-level.

Technical College. An alternative name for a college of further education, originally used extensively but now mainly confined to those colleges clearly identified with a town or self-contained area.

Technical High School. The Norwood Report of 1943 proposed three types of secondary school offering three types of curriculum. That of the grammar school would pursue knowledge 'for its own sake'; that of the technical high school 'would be closely related to industry, trades and commerce'; that of what became the secondary modern school 'would make a direct appeal to interests, which it would awaken by practical touch with affairs'. Some central or technical grammar schools had been established in the 1930s, and served as a model for the proposed technical high schools. But they failed to catch on in the post-war years, being seen as second best to grammar schools. Thus the tripartite system advocated by the Norwood Committee and supported by the Ministry of Education (although not specified by the 1944 Education Act) became increasingly bipartite, even in the areas where technical high schools had been introduced.

Technician Education Council (TEC). An independent body established in 1973 to develop 'schemes of technical education for persons at all levels of technician occupations in industry and elsewhere'. It awards qualifications at two levels. TEC Certificate and Diploma courses correspond roughly to Ordinary National Certificate and Diploma courses (q.v.), the diploma programmes being broader than those for the certificate. The TEC Higher Certificate and Diploma courses correspond to the level of Higher National courses. It has close liaison with BEC (q.v.), and its courses have a modular structure (q.v.).

Tertiary college. A college which provides post-16 education (q.v.) for a whole area or community within a single institution. All its courses are offered under further education regulations (q.v.), but some (notably A-level courses) will also be offered in schools and sixth-form colleges (q.v.) under schools regulations.

Tertiary Education. A term sometimes used to describe 16–19 education, and sometimes extending to higher education. It is used here to mean full and part-time education for 16–19 students, and for those adult students joining in courses primarily taken by 16–19 students.

University. An autonomous body undertaking degree and post-degree work in higher education, and awarding its own qualifications.

BIBLIOGRAPHY

BENN, C. (1978) '16–19. Wanted; a new will', *Forum*, autumn.

BENN, C. and SIMON, B. (1972) *Half Way There*, Penguin Books.

BRIGGS, ASA (Lord) (1978) 'Tuning in to the right band on the network', *The Guardian*, 24 October.

BUSINESS EDUCATION COUNCIL (1977) *BEC General Awards: Course Specification*.

CANTOR, L. and ROBERTS, I. (1972) *Further Education in England and Wales*, Routledge and Kegan Paul.

CENTRAL ADVISORY COUNCIL FOR EDUCATION (England) (1959) *15–18* (Crowther Report), HMSO.

CHOPPIN, B. and FARA, P. (1972) *Admission to Higher Education, A Select Annotated Bibliography*, NFER.

CHOPPIN, B. and ORR, L. (1976) *Aptitude Testing at Eighteen-Plus*, NFER.

CHRISTIE, T. and OLIVER, R. (1969) 'Academic performance at age 18-plus as related to school organisation', *Research in Education*, 2, Manchester University Press.

CITY AND GUILDS OF LONDON INSTITUTE (1978) *Foundation for a Career*.

COUNCIL FOR NATIONAL ACADEMIC AWARDS (1974) *Reflections on the Design of Modular Courses*.

COUNCIL FOR SCIENTIFIC POLICY (1968) *Enquiry into the Flow of Candidates in Science and Technology into Higher Education* (Dainton Report), HMSO.

CROWTHER REPORT, *see* Central Advisory Council.

DAINTON REPORT, *see* Council for Scientific Policy.

DEAN, J, and CHOPPIN, B. (1977) *Educational Provision 16–19*, NFER.

DEAN, J., BRADLEY, K., CHOPPIN, B. and VINCENT, D. (1979) *The Sixth Form and its Alternatives*, NFER.

DEPARTMENT OF EDUCATION AND SCIENCE: (1975) Survey 21, *Curricular Differences for Boys and Girls*, HMSO. (1977) *Curriculum 11–16*, DES.

DOE, R. and HADDOCK, K. (1978) 'Foundation for a life?', *The Times Educational Supplement*, 24 November.

DUCKWORTH, D. (1979) *The Continuing Swing? Pupils' Reluctance to Study Science*, NFER.

EDWARDS, A. D. (1970) *The Changing Sixth Form in the Twentieth Century*, Routledge and Kegan Paul.

FOGELMAN, K. (1972) *Leaving the Sixth Form: A Selection of Opinions*, NFER.

FURTHER EDUCATION CURRICULUM REVIEW AND DEVELOPMENT UNIT (1979) *Basis for Choice*, DES.

GORDON, P. and LAWTON, D. (1978) *Curriculum Change in the Nineteenth and Twentieth Centuries*, Hodder and Stoughton.

HEADMASTERS' ASSOCIATION (1968) *The Sixth Form of the Future.*

HEARNDEN, A. (1973) *Paths to University: Preparation, Assessment, Selection,* Macmillan.

HIRST, P. H. (1965) 'Liberal education and the nature of knowledge', in R. Archambault (ed), *Philosophical Analysis and Education,* Routledge.

HIRST, P. H. (1973) 'Towards a logic of curriculum development' in P. Taylor and J. Walton (eds), *The Curriculum: Research, Innovation and Change,* Ward Lock Educational.

HOLLAND, G. (1978) 'Help where it counts', *The Times Educational Supplement,* 14 April.

HOLMAN, D. (1977) *Cricklade—One Tertiary College,* Cricklade College, Andover, Hants.

HOLT, M. (1979) *Regenerating the Curriculum,* Routledge and Kegan Paul.

JANES, F. (1979) 'Creating a tertiary college from scratch', *Education,* 4 May.

JANES, F. and MILES, J. (1978) *Tertiary Colleges 1978,* Tertiary College Panel.

JUDGE, H. (1974) *School Is Not Yet Dead,* Longman.

KEOHANE REPORT, THE (1979) *Proposals for a Certificate of Extended Education,* HMSO.

KING, E. (1976) 'The educational needs of the 16–19 group', *Trends in Education,* June.

KING, E., MOOR, C. and MUNDY, J. (1975) *Post-Compulsory Education II: The Way Ahead,* Sage Publications.

KING, R. (1976) *School and College,* Routledge and Kegan Paul.

KING, R. WEARING (1968) *The English Sixth Form College,* Pergamon.

LACEY, C. (1970) *Hightown Grammar,* Manchester University Press.

LACK, G. (1967) 'The schools' response', *Schools Council Working Paper 12,* HMSO.

LAWTON, D. (1973) *Social Change, Educational Theory and Curriculum Planning,* Hodder and Stoughton.

MACFARLANE, E. (1978) *Sixth-Form Colleges,* Heinemann.

MACLURE, S. (1965) *Educational Documents, England and Wales,* Chapman and Hall.

MACLURE, S. (1975) 'The Schools Council and examinations' in R. Bell (ed.) *The Schools Council: a Second Look,* Ward Lock.

MERFIELD, P. (1973) 'The Exeter scheme', *Forum,* spring.

MILES, H. B. (1979) *Some Factors Affecting Attainment at 18–plus: A Study of Examination Performance in British Schools,* Pergamon.

OECD (1976) *Beyond Compulsory Schooling: Options and Changes in Upper Secondary Education,* OECD Paris.

OECD (1979) *Policies for Apprenticeship,* OECD Paris.

OWEN, J. (1977) 'Schools Council: a beginning, a middle, and now?', *The Times Educational Supplement,* 17 June.

PEDLEY, R. (1973) 'School or college?' *Education and Training*, July.

PEDLEY, R. (1977) *Towards the Comprehensive University*, Macmillan.

PERCIVAL, A. C. (1969) *The Origins of the Headmasters' Conference*, John Murray.

PETERSON, A. D. C. (1960) *Arts and Science Sides in the Sixth Form*, Oxford University Department of Education.

PETERSON, A. D. C. (1973) *The Future of the Sixth Form*, Routledge and Kegan Paul.

PHENIX, P. H. (1964) *Realms of Meaning*, McGraw Hill.

REID, W. (1972) *The Universities and the Sixth Form Curriculum*, Macmillan.

RUTTER, M., MAUGHAN, B., MORTIMORE, P. and OUSTON, J. (1979) *Fifteen Thousand Hours*, Open Books.

SCHOOLS COUNCIL:

(1966) *Working Paper 5: Sixth Form Curriculum and Examinations* HMSO.

(1967) *Working Paper 16: Some Further Proposals for Sixth Form Work*, HMSO.

(1969) *Working Paper 25: General Studies 16–18*, Evans/Methuen.

(1970) *Sixth Form Pupils and Teachers* (Sixth Form Survey Vol I), Books for Schools.

(1972) *Working Paper 45. 16–19: Growth and Response*, Evans/Methuen.

(1973) *The Examination Courses of First-Year Sixth Formers*, Macmillan.

(1978) *Examinations Bulletin 38. Examinations at 18–plus? Resource Implications of an N and F Curriculum and Examination Structure*, Evans/Methuen.

(1978) *Working Paper 60. Examinations at 18–plus: the N and F Studies*. Evans/Methuen.

(1979) *The N and F Debate: a Progress Report*, Schools Council Publications.

SECONDARY HEADS ASSOCIATION (1979) 'Staffing and curriculum in 11–16 schools', *SHA Review*, July.

SIMON, B. (1978) Editorial, *Forum*, autumn.

SKILBECK, M. (1975) 'School-based curriculum development' in E. Adams (ed.) *In-Service Education and Teachers' Centres*, Pergamon.

SKINNER, J. (1978) 'Some curriculum issues in higher education', *Cambridge Journal of Education*, lent.

STANDING CONFERENCE ON UNIVERSITY ENTRANCE (1978) *Universities and the N and F Proposals*.

STENHOUSE, L. (1975) *An Introduction to Curriculum Development*, Heinemann.

TAYLOR, P., REID, W. and HOLLEY, B. (1974) *The English Sixth Form*, Routledge and Kegan Paul.

TECHNICIAN EDUCATION COUNCIL (1974) Policy Statement.

VINCENT, D. and DEAN, J. (1977) *One-Year Courses in Colleges and Sixth Forms*, NFER.

WANKOWSKI, J. (1974) 'Teaching method and academic success in sixth form and university', *Journal of Curriculum Studies*, 6, 1.

WESTON, P. (1977) *Framework for the Curriculum*, NFER.

WHITE, J. (1973) *Towards a Compulsory Curriculum*, Routledge and Kegan Paul.

WHITFIELD, R. C. (1971) *Disciplines of the Curriculum*, McGraw Hill.

WHITFIELD, R. C. (ed) (1976) *International Baccalaureate Theory of Knowledge Course: Syllabus and Teachers' Notes*, Aston Educational Enquiry Monograph 2, University of Aston, Birmingham: on behalf of the IB Office, Geneva. (A revised version of these notes for use with UK students will be available as Monograph 10 from Aston in late 1979).

WHITFIELD, R. C. (1979) *Preparation for Family Responsibility*, National Children's Home.

WILLIAMS, R. (1961) *The Long Revolution*, Penguin Books.

Index